CONNECT

AND WORK WITH

SPIRIT
GUIDES

Shannon Yrizarry is a certified yoga teacher and professional clairvoyant who has written extensively in the wellness field. She teaches meditation and leads workshops on transforming the physical and emotional self through living a yogic lifestyle. She is also a certified Reiki practitioner and has done astrology readings, dream interpretations, and tarot for celebrities and television.

CONNECT
AND WORK WITH
SPIRIT
GUIDES

*Meet, Heal, and Manifest
with Your Divine Teachers*

SHANNON YRIZARRY

Llewellyn Publications
Woodbury, Minnesota

FIRST EDITION
First Printing, 2022

Book design by Rebecca Zins
Cover design by Kevin R. Brown
Illustration on page 22 by Mary Ann Zapalac
Illustration on page 96 by Llewellyn Art Department

Llewellyn is a registered trademark of Llewellyn Worldwide Ltd.

Library of Congress Cataloging-In-Publication Data
Pending
ISBN 978-0-7387-6938-7

Llewellyn Publications
A Division of Llewellyn Worldwide Ltd.
2143 Wooddale Drive
Woodbury, MN 55125-2989

www.llewellyn.com
Printed in the United States of America

I asked the leaf whether it was scared because it was autumn and the other leaves were falling. The leaf told me, "No. During the whole spring and summer I was completely alive. I worked hard to help nourish the tree, and much of me is in the tree. I am not limited by this form. I am also the whole tree, and when I go back to the soil, I will continue to nourish the tree. So I don't worry at all. As I leave this branch and float to the ground, I will wave to the tree and tell her, 'I will see you again very soon.'"

... after a while, I saw the leaf leave the branch and float down to the soil, dancing joyfully, because as it floated it saw itself already there in the tree. It was so happy. I bowed my head, knowing that I have a lot to learn from that leaf.

—Thich Nhat Hanh,
Peace Is Every Step

Disclaimer

This is a book for your creative and spiritual exploration. It is not meant to treat or cure any serious mental health conditions. If you are feeling anxious, depressed, or lonely, it is recommended to work with a mental health provider.

Contents

8 How to Further Develop Your Work with Spirit Guides 167

Acknowledgments

I would like to give my deep thanks to Lori Board Camacho, who channeled her clairvoyant training program fearlessly for me and so many other students. Her connection to her guide Raina was essential in my ability to help many people as a conduit between the physical and spiritual worlds.

I'd also like to thank my dear friend and gifted medium Afimaye Galarraga, who has been a spiritual anchor for me in my process of writing and saw these books I'd write before I started working on them. His conviction, commitment, and gifts have amplified my own work and allowed me to grow to continue to help others.

I'd like to thank medium Apryl Nicole for helping me see how to be open in public about the spirit world with her online live streams connecting to spirits without holding back.

I also want to thank my friends from Awakenings Metaphysical Center in Laguna Hills, California: Maylynne Graves, Diana Wint, Brandon Camacho, Michael Mayo, and Amanda Mehalick.

I'd also like to thank my friends from House of Intuition in Los Angeles: Mary Grisey, Kristin Mothersbaugh, Marcy Vargas, Alex Vargas, Marlene Vargas, Jaakko Manninen, Naha Armady, and Christine Aprile.

There are many more who I have worked with throughout my career as a professional psychic and who have stood by my side to bring this important spiritual realm and multidimensional truth back to modern society. Your work is inspiring to me, and even though we are separated by distance, I follow your posts and see your brave work.

Introduction

*Y*ou can greatly benefit from meeting and working with your spirit guides. You can ask them for advice, get inspiration to change your life, and feel supported at all times. Truly, they are waiting to be your very best friends. This easy guide will help you understand the spirit world and how to develop the ability to contact the guides waiting to assist you in all areas of life. Working with spirit guides makes life magical and takes away many fears that can come with living in a society disconnected from the spirit world. Drawing on personal experiences that are both surprising and eye-opening, the book will help you step-by-step as you awaken your innate spiritual connection to high-vibrational guides.

Here I will help answer many questions you have about the spirit world and address misconceptions and cultural perspectives that often stop people from developing relationships with their spiritual allies. As you progress through the book, you will work on this skill with meditations and reflective journal exercises. You will start out by learning about the energy in your body. Next you will learn meditations to connect with your guides. This part is all about creating a regular targeted meditation practice. You will then develop a relationship with your own higher self and get to meet the spirit guides who are ready to help you. Along the way there are explanations to help you really know why each step is taken.

Once you understand how to work with other-dimensional beings—how they can show up and how they communicate with you—you will be able to work on manifesting, healing, and helping others with this ability. This book will show you how it is easy to develop this spiritual gift. As you work through the exercises, I will walk you through the things that will come up, removing the mystery and making contacting guides a normal part of your life, as it has been in many more spiritually based cultures.

For those already diving into psychic development and intuition, this material will help you expand your abilities. By working with spirit guides, you will have access to new ideas, information, and assistance that will help you be a stronger psychic. If you are on the path of a healer or think you might want to pursue it, you can use this book to anchor your skills and hone in on this aspect of psychic development. You will experience the spiritual dimension that has been written about for so long. This will help you really know that the spirit world is working with us, helping humanity. You will know how to connect with your guides to help you with the most difficult experiences.

How to Use This Book

This book is designed to take you from step one all the way to a very strong connection with your spirit guides. There are meditations to start you out, and they include journaling exercises to reflect on and record this deeply transformational process. You can either get a dedicated journal and special pen for this work or keep a digital journal on your phone or computer if you feel like that is more your style. Just make sure you have a designated place to capture the insights that are going to show up and use the powerful writing prompts.

You will benefit from making a designated space for the meditations in this book. That may be a place in the park or the most comfortable place in your room. You want a place that feels calm.

The pace you take with this book is up to you. It will be inspiring for you to see the changes as you really digest and integrate each chapter into your life. Try to approach each chapter with your full focus and a sense of wonder about this sacred process so you engage deeply with the topic and meditation. To keep you motivated and moving forward, you'll find many tips on how to handle common roadblocks that come up. This is a very exciting moment as you are about to see the iceberg beneath the water that is full of magic!

1

What Spirit Guides Are and How They Can Help You

Welcome to a gateway to your soul, your higher self, and your spirit guides. This book will be an energy portal for you to solve some of the deepest questions and issues you face in your life. It will help you understand the secrets of the spirit world and allow you to tap into energy that will change your life in infinitely positive ways. This will help you create a strong foundation to do your spiritual work and heal on many levels. If you've felt for years like you wanted to deepen your spiritual connection but really didn't know where to start, it is my sincere and deepest intention that this book will offer that safe haven and refuge to get you to that space.

The great thing is, you do not have to subscribe to any belief system or let go of any religious practice in order to really grasp and work with the exercises in this book. This is for everyone and requires no blind following of any leader or guru. This book allows you to be in the driver's seat of your spiritual development, which will subsequently put you in control of your life in ways you may not yet conceive. The way to the soul is paved with many who have walked the path and want to help you, both on this physical side and on the other side. Take a moment to set your intention to develop a sacred connection to your soul through this book and follow your heart, trust your intuition, and experience the true loving magic of spirit guides that are waiting to meet you.

Sometimes I will bring up examples from my experience with guides to help explain a concept. Your experiences should not and will not be the same as mine. There is no limit to the type of relationship and wonderful and magical ways you will experience your guides. Try not to compare your process to mine because it is best to stay in a state of excited and relaxed trust that your journey will be exactly what you need. I have often found myself envisioning my life becoming like the teachers that I looked up to or learned a lot from, but realize that just as each fingerprint is somehow entirely unique, so is our own journey to our soul and with our spiritual guides that can work with us in infinite ways. So whether your guides choose to make you aware of colors in your environment and communicate with you that way, pop songs into your head to get a message through, or show up as a wise elder, don't judge it; just relax and stay in a state of receptiveness, which will allow you to have the childlike first-time experience mind necessary to start perceiving other layers of energy.

We will be going over all the concepts, common questions, exciting things to look forward to, and the steps you need to take on this journey. You have found something that can very well be a turning point, where you will look back and realize how, from this moment, things became more magical, you became more alive, and happiness continued to be found in greater quantities, with more of a real sense that it is and can be your permanent state.

An Introduction to the Concept of Spirit Guides

When you hear the term "spirit guide," different ideas may flash in your head depending on what you've heard and how much you've been exposed to the topic. Those flashes of memories may be very vivid or somewhat vague, and either way, you are going to get a much deeper and more visceral experience of them—you will have more than ideas because you're going to have actual encounters! Let's look at what a spirit guide is. The real truth of what a spirit guide is is in the name itself. It is a consciousness that is there to guide you. It is not just a spirit but a benevolent one that shows up to help you.

Spirit guides have been part of human life for a very long time; they are in our collective memory. Let's break down the concept itself. Spirit guides are more than an inspiring idea or invisible friend that we conjure in our imagination, similar to how a writer creates characters to tell a story. They are conscious beings that are not in bodies. They are not limited by being in a body and do not need food or sleep. They can assist you instantaneously as they are in other dimensions where linear time does not exist. Spirit guides can be former human spirits, a group of spirits, beings from other star systems, or inhuman spirits that are pure consciousness. They may reveal a name, be genderless, and show up as a lifelong companion or come and go as needed. Their purpose is to help humanity evolve, with the ultimate goal of peace, love, and unification of consciousness.

Now let's look at what the concept of a spirit guide includes. The term "spirit animal" is something that lives under the category of spirit guide but is not nearly the only thing that a spirit guide can be. A spirit guide is not a physical being, although it may have been one at some point. For example, the spirit of a saint can become a spirit guide. However, spirit guides are often not former human spirits and sometimes are a group of spirits or have no real human-like qualities at all. While our ancestors can become strong spirit guides in our life, not all of them do.

Spirit guides can be angels. Angels tend to offer support without back-and-forth communication. Each spirit guide offers a different type of assistance and communication. Angels help with energy as buffers in our emotional and electromagnetic fields, kind of like crystals, whereas other spirit guides are more specific personalities with the ability to communicate to us in words, and instead of asking for their assistance, as we do with angels, our relationship with spirit guides is much more about learning from them.

Spirit guides can also be certain deities/gods/goddesses, but often a deity is a group consciousness projected by people and fed by people; thus it does not have its own reasoning capabilities that it can use its discernment with to proffer advice. Spirit guides are often very wise spirits that have evolved over many lifetimes in different realms of existence. They offer advice that will allow you know deeper truths about the nature of reality. They will help you shift your perspective, which will empower you. This happens as they help you experience an energetic web beyond what the mind usually perceives.

Often deities are strong energy fields that people tap into to reach a desired state. For example, the energy of Lakshmi helps people get into the frequency of abundance because so much mental energy has been poured into this concept. If that is a little too deep for you at this point, don't worry about it. You will get all the clear and concise instructions and easy practices you need to fully grasp these differences. It may help you to come back and reread this introduction as you go through this book, as this is likely a completely new type of information for you to process, with many new terms. By the end of the book you will have learned the different players in the spiritual dimensions.

Working with spirit guides is not to be taken lightly and should be approached with guidance, reverence, and some knowledge of the spirit world. You will learn how to meditate in a deep state before you start to connect with a spirit guide. You will learn about your own energy system and specific ways to create meditative states. The process will allow you to heal energy within yourself that you need to release in order to raise your vibration to meet your guides. The journey of meeting your guides requires humility and being willing to let go of some of the ideas you have that are fear-based and keep you from tapping into the spirit world. These fears and negative emotions will be addressed, and you'll be able to work on them further as you progress. Subsequent chapters will give you a firm grasp of living with spirit guides in a symbiotic state.

Where Spirit Guides Have Been Documented Throughout History

Peruvian and Native American shamans represent some of the ancient cultures that have been contacting spirit guides for thousands of years. It is estimated that Native Americans inhabited North America for about 20,000 years before it was settled by Europeans, and there is evidence that cultures existed in Peru as far back as 1,000 BCE, approximately 3,000 years ago. Shamans would often go to a mountaintop to contact their spirit guides, ancestors, and plant and animal spirits. They also carried a portable altar that helped them connect to their spirit guides. To this day, spiritual healers often bring their altar with them to assist them in contacting spirit guides. You will learn how to do this as well.

Spirit doctors from many different spiritual traditions in Africa connect to spirit guides, as do the Celtic shamans of Ireland. African religions, which are heavily reliant on looking to the spirits of ancestors and other spirits for guidance in life, date back way before Christian and Muslim faiths began influencing Africa. Humans are said to have been on the continent of Africa for 200,000 years. Fast forward to some more modern cultures and you have stories of angels and ascended masters such as Enoch in Christianity and Judaism. In the Bibles included in most American hotel and motel rooms, it is said Enoch was alive and walked with God.

In India Hindus have long had a polytheistic religion with female and male spirits, and Chinese Buddhists (also known as Han Buddhists) believe the spirits of humans live on and have different spirits in their culture that are connected to almost everything. Hinduism is 4,000 years old and Buddhism is 2,500 years old.

I could continue to recount how ancient cultures have relied on spirit guides as an integral part of daily life, but I think you get the point. People have and still are connecting to spirits, unless everyone has been hallucinating. Of course, these ancient systems are still alive today, and people continue to work with spirit guides. It will help you to know pretty much everyone, at different points, will find themselves asking what to do if they're not getting messages. That question has a few layers that I will unpack for you. No matter what you currently believe or don't believe, as you go through this book, you will gain a better understanding of spirit guides and how they can help you in your life. Yes, the spirit world allows you to be who you want to be—fancy that!

Practical Ways Spirit Guides Can Assist You

This book is designed to help you pick the fruit from your spiritual tree of gifts. Spirit guides are able to help you find greater levels of joy beyond what society can provide. Happy people tend to attract success! The ways spirit guides can help you enjoy life and become successful have an energetic root, and they work with our emotional side by creating more consistently positive emotional states.

Spirit guides help you extract the energy of your intention and create beautiful stories with it. They will help you find new perspectives on difficult situations in your life and feel the magic that can be felt even in a seemingly impossible scenario. They are the ticket to your silver lining in life now and in the future, as well as for healing the energy you carry from the past.

Yes, they are here to help your soul evolve after this life, but they are also helping you in the here and now, where you can raise your vibration to experience heaven on earth regardless of what you own, how popular you are, or what you've been through. They will help you reclaim your power by showing you how to heal your energy and create patterns that keep you in a high-vibration state. They can help you manifest by helping you understand the true energetic nature of the universe.

In a practical sense, they can help you heal your self-esteem, body image, attitude, and overall well-being, and they can help you treat yourself with the ultimate tender loving care. They can help you heal your relationships, find a sense of calm when things are up in the air, and help you through the toughest things like losing a loved one or struggling with health.

Spirit guides can help you make some of the hardest decisions of your life, and as you raise your vibration to work with them, those decisions will start to be revealed to you. I'm talking about the important stuff such as who you allow in your life, whose opinions you choose to let affect your life, what values you embrace, and how you can open your spiritual gifts. Those deep core-level choices never may have seemed like choices before, which is why raising your vibration to connect with your guides is a process of awakening and freedom.

Here are just some of the many practical ways building a relationship with your spirit guides can help you:

Build Trust in Yourself

Like a teacher, a guide can show up to help you see the energy you've been feeding that makes you fear your own decision-making. When we don't trust ourselves, we think that we need to ask other people about what we should do with our lives and how to sculpt the vision for our futures. Spirit guides can show you a deeper, more fulfilling vision by helping you tap into new frequencies where you're able to see what life would feel like when you trust yourself.

This isn't about trusting your reasoning and logic; this is about trusting your spiritual truth, the dream that has always been alive in your heart that people often will tell you is foolish. You really cannot put a monetary value on just how different your life will be when you're able to trust you have a spiritual self beyond your body that is real.

Guides can help you do this by speaking the language of feelings through images, memories, symbols, colors, and sounds. They will guide you to find a state of relaxation where the usual things that seem so important and stress you out are simply nonexistent. They help you see the big picture, where your soul wants you to be a part of helping humanity evolve instead of just trying to fulfill the ego's primal instinct to procreate, seek pleasure, and feel important, which leaves us feeling empty. They will help you see these egoistic patterns as pointless uses of time and precious energy so that you can align with goals that will actually make you happy.

13

Create the Life of Your Dreams

Spirit guides can help you work on releasing fears by shifting your focus to more loving, compassionate vibrations. These beings are so loving that they can help you create a bridge in your mind to be able to perceive the path to get from where you are to where you want to be. They help us get in touch with a deeper sense of motivation that is not created from our environment but that comes from a space that looks out for the betterment of all. They help us see how our energy expands and strengthens when we listen to what our own intuition urges us to do.

By getting us in touch with a new sense of motivation, they are tapping us into a well of energy that is stronger than what we had before. That energy allows us to mentally compute at a faster rate so that we can see more resources available to us in order to create the life of our dreams. Our creative instincts are stronger, and we start connecting the dots to get where we want to go with their help. They are opening energetic doors that allow us to see how to adjust the little decisions in our life that block our energy such as how we eat, sleep, drink, and communicate. This allows us to create a snowball effect of positive energy and an avalanche of success. By helping us tap into self-love and enhance the connection to the identity of our soul, they help us break toxic ties to fear-based habits of living a life that is "safe" or that fits the mold so we can turn on our creative power.

Redefine Success

When you meet your spirit guides, you will always feel their energy, which is one way they teach you. In the altered state you will learn to reach to be able to communicate with your spirit guides, you'll sense the joy and freedom that is their natural state. This will reveal to you a new, expanded level of happiness that you can cultivate in your life. Once you experience their consciousness, the fleeting feelings brought by monetary or social status will pale in comparison, easily allowing you to align your definition of success to something you've experienced as the ultimate state of happiness.

Just as your guides enjoy helping you get to this state of mind, you will naturally find joy from helping others also free their minds of fear and more superficial definitions of success. This is often why you see people who are just awakening trying to enthusiastically get everyone to meditate with them. However, your guides will also show you over time that you do not need to spark every soul's awakening; you can't, and often our ego is still going through a deconditioning phase when we try to come up with schemes to be the one to bring this wisdom to the masses. The wisdom they will show you is that you do not have to frantically try to change everyone and become successful by society's standards as a spiritual savant. You need only resonate a high state of mind to positively impact the world and allow the path to be revealed that your soul is meant to traverse.

They will creatively show you where you aren't willing to put in the energy to contribute to your soul's purpose in order to empower you to take responsibility for your own energy. They have the ability to communicate extremely complex ideas to us through a simple image, song, feeling, or word that processes on an energetic level and allows us to know much deeper truths about the nature of reality, happiness, and the universe. Often they help us face our fear of death, which is constructed when we think our identity is just the ego. That very fear is often what creates our subconscious motivations to cling to the physical world.

Experience Deep Happiness

Your guides will help release the habits from your mind that keep you fretting over the future or past. In the altered state you will be in to meet them, you will be extremely present—perhaps more present than you have ever been. This will allow you to experience the unity of consciousness of all creation, where time is a construct and reality itself is constantly re-creating itself. The vastness of this energetic connection and richness of this experience will allow you to reach such a deep state of happiness that you will continue to seek the experience of being present without the stories of the mind that block us from this level of freedom.

Your guides will help you see how you can experience this altered state by drawing your attention to things that get you into that state of mind such as certain physical activities, creative processes, and even simple household tasks. They may urge you to leave big stressful jobs that keep you wound up so that you can find a more peaceful job that allows you to experience this more relaxed, peaceful state. As you work with your guides, you'll start to understand the happy, spiritually woowoo people who talk about energy, carry a drum, and love to put on essential oils. You'll start to see the draw of the Grateful Dead and the allure of a simple light show or peaceful nature setting. You'll seek out peace and presence more than image and prestige. You'll start to find new hobbies that bring about this state, surround yourself with people who are good at living in it, and avoid people who pull you further away from it until your mind is an impenetrable compound of pure bliss.

See all that you have to look forward to? And don't worry—this doesn't mean you will lose touch with reality. You will only gain a deeper understanding of the true nature of reality, which will encourage you to lose the parts that don't provide energetic sustenance. As your new definition of success will become cheaper, your new way to experience deeper levels of happiness will as well. They will both also become more simple, allowing you to take the pressure off of yourself to be perfect by society's standards.

Set Healthy Boundaries

The cool thing about being present with your guides and getting used to that high-vibe state is that it also allows you to be super intuitive. This means you will get insider's info about someone's true intentions so that you can avoid toxic jobs, relationships, family members, schemes, and entire industries that could lead to problems, fights, depression, addiction, and abuse. Your guides allow you to play in a state of bliss, showing you that you can live in it when you keep your vibes, thoughts, and emotions positive and loving. This approach to creating healthy boundaries is a positive reward system instead of the way you may have tried in the past, which feels like cutting yourself off from something you want. Instead of feeling like you're starving yourself of the good stuff, you will easily remove the things that don't serve your energetic growth.

For those of us who have looked for happiness in the bottom of a bottle, in the arms of a lover that we know is all wrong for us, or through the insatiable pursuit of recognition, these new boundaries will come much more effortlessly and actually stick. Spirit guides help us see the energy a person has so we choose partners based on their kindness and not how they help bolster our self-esteem. They can help us break toxic patterns of dating abusive people or having them in our lives so we can make room for those who will treat us well. The ability to make shifts like this stems from the relationship with your spirit guides that helps you heal internally and then allows your world to reflect that healing back to you.

Release Negative Energy for Good

Not only will having these spiritual allies help you lose interest in bad habits and bad people, they will help you create more positive habitual ways of thinking that are compassionate, loving, and trusting that you're always going to be fine. They help you get much more in tune with your intuitive side, which doesn't steer you wrong and allows you to embrace all stages, unexpected turns, personal challenges, and emotions with love so that no outside experience can steal your happiness or state of peace.

Heal Physically

One of my spirit guides shows up as a Native woman from South America. She has a unique relationship with me in that she only gives me the name of herbs and plants that I need for healing. In one instance, I had been in and out of the doctor's office after four months of lung pain. She told me to get mullein, which I hadn't heard of. When I looked it up, it was for bronchial health, and it started me on the process of healing. Soon after, I went to the doctor and after a cardiograph, chest X-ray, blood tests, and multiple visits, it was surmised that I had had bronchitis for four months, and I was able to get the proper medications. Without this spirit guide's help, I don't think I would have thought to go to the doctor because I assumed it was COVID-19 and I couldn't do anything about it.

Getting to Know Your Energy Field

Welcome to the first step in meeting your spirit guides! Before you sit down to meditate, we are going to go over what your energy field is. This will help you understand why you need to meditate in order to meet your spirit guides and how maintaining your energy field will help you connect to your spirit guides.

Within both the Hindu chakra system and the ancient Chinese meridian system, there are general similarities that make it beyond reasonable doubt that we have an energy field. Martial artists and yogis work with the energy field to bring about certain abilities such as harnessing chi to move through objects or propel them as well as see the future and see remotely. By balancing their energy field, strengthening it, raising the vibration of it, and then directing the energy within it, they are able to perform what to the layperson seems like superhuman feats.

The first thing to know is that around you is essentially a bubble of energy that is constantly interacting with the environment, both taking in energy and giving it. The bubble of energy around you—your aura—is also exchanging information with energy centers and channels that move within your body (the chakras and meridians). Although you can't see the aura, chakras, or meridians, you will be able to feel them. For example, when someone with a large aura enters a room, you notice them and so does everyone else. People we barely notice are either intentionally pulling their energy in or they have low energy and a small aura. When our auras interact, we get an intuitive download on the type of person we are meeting. You've probably noticed that certain people seem really kind and warm while others feel jumpy and untrustworthy; that is all information you pick up from the aura.

In order to meet your spirit guides, you will learn techniques to clear the aura of low vibrations so you can meet your very high-vibration guides. That way, even if you live or work with low-vibration people who are mucking up your aura, you'll still be able to have a steady working relationship with your guides! The other communication line that is really important is opening the flow of energy through the upper chakras to the crown chakra. This top chakra is the highest vibration, so it is the access point to your spirit guides.

If you're feeling a bit lost right now, that would be completely normal. Let me break down some of this a little bit more so that you can visualize what I'm talking about.

Think of each chakra as a spinning vortex, much like the time machine Austin Powers jumps into to go back to the '60s. You have seven of those in your body that interact with your aura, picking up and giving out energetic imprints and charges. Each one has a specific frequency that it runs optimally at and correlates to emotions that are also at that frequency. To keep things simple, let's just say that anger is a low-vibe frequency that might have a wavelength of 5 hertz, while love is a stronger vibration that could be 25 hertz. In order to raise our frequency, we must raise our vibrational state. In order to stay in a high-frequency state, we must maintain a positive emotional state. Training ourselves to think positive will help us access the top chakra (crown chakra), which is the portal to our spirit guides. The exercises in this book will take you through this process step-by-step.

Just as the time machine in the Austin Powers movie needed electricity to turn on, the chakras need energy too. When we are focused on who made us mad, worried about what to do over the weekend, or stressing about how we look, we are not sending any energy to the crown chakra, which is where we need energy in order to tap into the spiritual dimensions. Directing energy requires us to be able to focus, and then the higher laws of the universe start to help us out. Our mind is actually able to direct our energy. I experienced this when I became Reiki certified and the instructor taught us to focus on the palms of our hands, which started to feel as though they were buzzing and electrified. It was a huge eye-opening experience of energy that you too will be able to experience at the top of your head when it starts to tingle and buzz.

The Chakras

Your body has major energy centers called chakras that are the crossroads of energy in your body. Think of them as the major freeways that get lots of traffic and can get backed up because of it. Each of these major intersections can help you get to the frequency you need in order to contact your guides. You will learn how to maintain the flow of traffic in these intersections in order to get your energy up to the top of your head, where the connection to your guides lives. You'll actually start your work with guides and continue it daily using a chakra-clearing meditation.

First, let's take a look at these major energy centers and get friendly with them. It's easier to work with something when you have a bit of information about what it does, and this will help you recognize if there's a major area in your life blocking you from connecting to your guides. If one chakra isn't flowing, none of the others are full-speed either.

THE SEVEN CHAKRAS

There are seven major chakras. We will include the aura (the energy field around our body) as the eighth chakra.

First Chakra

The first chakra is called the root chakra. It vibrates at the frequency of red, meaning red can help activate it. It is located at the base of the spinal column. When it's flowing, you feel energetic, safe, and like you can provide for yourself. When it's stuck, blown out, or shrunken, it means energy is not moving back and forth as it should, and you may feel scared, overeat, hoard things, hold on to money too much, and feel like you're tired or don't belong. Someone who has a blockage here may have trouble paying their bills, be overweight, experience chronic fatigue, or be obsessed with making more money.

Second Chakra

The second chakra is called the sacral chakra. It vibrates at the frequency of orange, so that color can help activate it. It is located at the reproductive organs. When it's healthy, you have no trouble expressing your desires, manifesting, having healthy intimacy, and feeling your emotions without trying to snuff them out. When it's unhealthy, you lack creativity, develop addictions to substances, are either afraid of or obsessed with sex, and possibly feel no emotions. Someone with an energy issue here may find they drink to deal with their problems, which only causes more of them, but they feel out of control with their impulse to drink. Someone may also worry they have no personal power because they don't see they have the ability to create.

Third Chakra

The third chakra is called the solar plexus chakra. It vibrates at the frequency of yellow, and that color can activate it. If this energy center, which is located at the top of the stomach, is healthy, it will allow you to feel joyful, optimistic, and confident. This energy center also allows you to have a sense of humor. If you feel pessimistic, timid, self-conscious, controlling, aggressive, or self-obsessed, this chakra is not flowing properly. Notice how the first three conditions would represent an underactive chakra and the last three reveal an overactive chakra. Thus, when you have too little of what a chakra's function is, it has too little energy, while having excess traits of that chakra means it has too much energy.

Fourth Chakra

The fourth chakra is called the heart chakra. And you guessed it: it's located at the heart area. If you don't know what color it's linked to yet, close your eyes and see what color comes to mind when you focus your attention there. If you saw green, your intuition was right. That color can help heal and activate this chakra. If you feel like your life is moving forward, you have deep relationships, and you are independent, compassionate, self-loving, and able to share and receive love, this chakra is doing its job. If it's shrunken, blocked, or swollen, you may feel sadness, codependency, jealousy, grief, or real heartache. Someone who has an energy imbalance here may give too much and not know when to stop.

Fifth Chakra

The fifth chakra, which is very connected to your ability to communicate with your spirit guides, is called the throat chakra. It is located at the neck and mouth and resonates with the color blue, which will help heal and energize it. If it's flowing and doing well, you will speak clearly and directly without speaking over people or lying. You will also be able to hear and share what your guides want to communicate to you. When this chakra isn't functioning, you'll have trouble saying how you feel and won't be able to enact your ideas. There is magic to this chakra because it creates sound, a vibration that interacts with the universe.

Sixth Chakra

The sixth chakra, located at the brow point, is called the third eye chakra. This is a high-vibrational chakra that helps you see the images that your guides wish to share with you. It resonates with the color purple. Wearing, visualizing, or surrounding yourself with purple will help bring energy to this area. Your guides can use this chakra to show you different times and dimensions, and this is the point of entry to your intuitive abilities. When healthy, this chakra leads to wisdom, vision, mental clarity, a good memory, and even good eyesight. When this chakra malfunctions, it sends off warning signs like headaches, earaches, or nasal congestion. You may also feel lost, confused, or paranoid.

Seventh Chakra

The seventh chakra, the crown chakra, is the chakra most people associate with spirit guides. It is the highest vibration of the seven chakras in the body, and it extends from the top of the head upward. It resonates with the color white or pink, and using these colors can help keep it open. When this chakra is doing well, you'll actually feel a sensation at the top of the head and have good hair growth as well as skin health. You'll also feel peaceful, have access to universal truths, and be able to contact the spirit guides you are destined to meet on your soul's journey. When this chakra is not functioning, oh boy, it's depressing. You will feel isolated and lonely and may have mental health issues and insomnia.

~

Many people have a closed heart chakra, which means they have never experienced what their life is like when the upper chakras are flowing. They live in their lower three chakras, which are more associated with the primal instincts of seeking money, sex, and power.

The eighth chakra is a big part of this ecosystem and links to all the chakras. It is through this chakra that you're constantly picking up information from your environment and funneling it into your other chakras. The daily meditations you will learn in this book will help you clean your aura so that you can get your vibration high enough to contact your helpful guides, who are excited to meet you!

The aura is gold but also has all the colors of the chakras within its layers when it's balanced. Just like highways are two-way streets, your own thoughts and emotions affect your aura and can fill it with heavy, dense, negative energy, which is why creating a lifestyle that is positive will aid in your goal of working with your guides.

Before we end this chapter, you are going to start your experience of working with your own energy. This simple meditation is not one that you need to do each time you contact your spirit guides, but for those who are not used to sensing energy, this may be something you want to practice until it becomes familiar.

To do the meditation, you can either lie down, sit in a chair with your feet flat on the ground, or sit on a cushion in a cross-legged position. When you meditate, it's important your spine is straight. Energy flows better through the central channel in the spinal column when it's straight. If your spine is out of alignment, which is usually indicated by pain, you will also have trouble accessing your guides. A simple remedy for that is to lie on your back and hug your knees to your chest, press your lower back into the floor, and suck in your stomach; holding that position, let go of your knees and lower your feet to the ground and back up about ten times. This often fixes subtle misalignments.

You also may want to play some soothing meditation music without heavy bass or lyrics. This helps you slip into a meditative state by cuing your mind to relax. Steven Halpern's meditation music is a great tool for meditation and is easy to find online. Turn off your phone alerts and make sure you won't be disturbed.

You may want to record this meditation and all of the meditations in this book as you get to them so that you can relax and meditate with your eyes closed. Speak slowly and leave space if the meditation instructs you to do something. Try to use a calming voice so it will help you relax.

~

It's time to start your empowering healing journey with spirit.

Take a slow deep breath in your nose, breathing deeper than you usually do. Slow the rate at which you exhale breathing out through your nose. Breathe gently but deeper than usual. Connecting to your guides will not be something you force or need to exert extreme energy doing. It is about getting relaxed and tuning into the subtle energy you are already feeling. This subtle energy will get much easier to sense soon. Allow a gentle smile to come over your face, knowing you're taking this step toward your spiritual growth.

Now bring your awareness to the surface of your skin. We are used to thinking of our identity in terms of our body but not in terms of our energy, which our body is made of. Imagine a light just at the surface of your skin around your entire body. This light is the light of your awareness, and it is a part of you because it is a part of your consciousness.

Now, as you breathe, with each inhale expand your awareness of this field of light slightly more around your body. You are just noticing the energy that is already there by bringing your awareness to it. Once you've taken a few more deep breaths, notice that you have expanded your awareness to the energy that is about a foot or two around you. This is your aura, the energy field that holds your emotional energy with the channels of energy in your body. This energy field is just as much a part of you as your mind and body are. Welcome to your spirit; like the proverbial tip of the iceberg, you're just meeting the first part of it. You are so vast, wise, creative, and capable. You will find that your spirit guides are going to help you get to know this part of yourself.

Now, to practice noticing the quality of your energy, just scan your energy field in your mind's eye (what you visualize with your eyes closed). Notice if anything stands out—even something that doesn't seem important is important. You may notice something your first time and you may not. Either way, you are doing great. After a few moments of just observing and breathing slowly, take a deep breath and bring yourself back to your normal alert state.

Great job completing your first meditation in the book! This is a great accomplishment on your journey, and I would celebrate it. If your critical mind is saying you didn't do it well enough or you won't ever get it, you can go ahead and let those thoughts go right now. You will get used to meditating the more you do it. Have you ever tried to just do fifty push-ups out of nowhere? It's practically impossible. You have to do a little more each day and build up to the point where it feels possible and *is* possible. Your ability to focus and enjoy meditation will come with time. Even if you feel like you had trouble focusing or couldn't sense your energy field today, go ahead and celebrate that you did try and that you're on your soul's path of healing. You are right where you need to be.

How to Overcome Doubt and Fear About Spirit Guides

*I*n this chapter we will address the most common doubts you probably have about the existence of spirit guides or your ability to have a valuable relationship with them. We will look at the root cause of those assumptions and how to address them so they don't stop you. This will empower you to see into your mind on a deeper level and understand how some of those subconscious ideas have been based on things people have said or things you may have seen on TV.

Then we will address the fear that many people deal with about contacting the spirit world and where that fear comes from. Fears are often instilled by people who are misinformed or subscribed to a belief system that has perpetuated fear of something it doesn't truly understand for many generations. We will address this in an easy-to-understand manner that will help you see how something you may have taken as absolute truth your whole life may actually be a fear-based story you're holding on to, not knowing there was another way to see things.

Also, I'll share with you some of my personal experiences in dealing with doubt and fear as I became a professional psychic and started working with my spirit guides to show you that it is very possible to overcome these common doubts and fears.

Why Most People Today Don't Know Spirit Guides Exist

In order to develop this skill, it is very helpful to understand why most people today don't know the truth about spirit guides. Before Christianity (and its largest branch, Roman Catholicism) became a dominant belief system, polytheistic religions and spiritual systems worked with the spirit world directly. A book (that has been made into a movie) that helps show this change is called *The Mists of Avalon*. Before the violent and deadly cleansing of people who challenged the faith of the papacy (the pope), women also were able to conduct spiritual services and were considered to be on an equal footing with men in the spiritual world. When the new system spread fear of anyone who contacted spirit directly, especially women, the gift of intuition became something that instilled fear of being literally burned to death.

The Roman Catholic Church's hierarchy of power—male priests, cardinals, and bishops—became the new dominating system where women were stripped of their power and also forced to denounce their spiritual practices of connecting to spirit guides to protect their families and children. Since then, there has been continual pressure from the many branches of Christianity that invoke fear and mistrust of anyone claiming they can contact God, angels, or spirits not listed in the Bible. This seals the power of their church, ensuring that the population pledges their 10 percent tithe to help absolve their sins—and perpetuating a very wealthy institution.

It also hasn't helped that psychics have had a culture of pushing people to spend money, instilling the fear that if they don't, something bad will befall them. The way that tarot readers and psychics have been portrayed as charlatans in the media is half true in that for a long time some people have misused their psychic abilities to swindle others, not realizing how harmful it was to approach the public in this way. By threatening people, it not only created mistrust of psychics and related topics, but it also stopped people from investigating topics for themselves.

The bad reputation of people who have not themselves worked in a high-vibrational state due to interests of personal gain, a lack of training, and perpetuated by a culture that lacked a better vision has made it so our subconscious is that much more afraid to even approach the topic of spirit guides lest someone see it in our search history. Growing up in the church, I remember being terrified if I even thought about spirits and the stories I had heard of them. I thought God could see that I was thinking about them and felt guilty for even wondering what they were. The fear spread by the institution as well as the actions of some psychics have given the whole topic a woefully misconstrued image and hidden the benefits of the spiritual realms from people who could be helped by the knowledge and experience.

35

Why You Have Doubts That It's All in Your Imagination

All of this backstory and societal conditioning has made most people hugely unaware that for much of human history, most humans have had a very strong and open connection to the spirit world. This is documented in all religious texts even if they promote fear of the spirit world. One of the biggest hindrances we come up against in the process of connecting to our guides is not believing what we experience. We are so conditioned to think that the things we see in our mind are pure imagination, we can't also hold the truth that we are actually experiencing a different dimension.

In a radio interview I did about my first book, I was asked how to tell if the information you're getting is real or imagined. This admittedly is one of the more challenging aspects of connecting to your guides, but I would recommend you don't let it stop you when it comes up. There is a way to get past it, and one of the best ways is to maintain the attitude that the fear of being wrong is not as important as continuing to do the work, nor is the doubt of imagining it worth focusing on or worrying about. You will actually be able to tell what is real and imagined because the vibration will seem different and the clarity or strength of the message will feel different too. This will be discussed further when we address how to bypass the ego in meditation by using your intention.

Why Does It Seem So Hard to Connect to Spirit Guides?

If you're asking yourself this question, it's important to know that you're asking the right questions, and feeling that way is completely normal given that most education about spiritual topics is hard to find and not widely known. I can assure you that it will get easier, especially after you get through this book. You can refer to chapter 5 if you're still not connecting with your guides after working through the other meditations, which can help you tighten some of the energetic nuts and bolts. For now, let's first address some of the most basic things we need to know in order to make connecting with guides easier.

Good news: you probably need to learn how to really relax. If you were raised to excel at everything you do, as most of us in suburban modern life are, chances are you really are legitimately bad at allowing yourself to relax. I'm talking about unstructured time where you're not trying to plan something or be productive and you are not talking or moving. This state of relaxation is actually the only way to access your spirit guides, and it's not the natural state for modern adults. Some people are just naturally calm, but most of us are stress balls who are competing, trying to better ourselves in the "real world," and constantly making ourselves busy but feeling like we don't have a choice. If you think back to the benefits of connecting to your spirit guides we went over in chapter 1, the motivation to relax regularly and deeply will be easier to find.

Relaxing daily will help you be healthier, happier, more creative, and easier to be around. The art of relaxation comes over time. You can enhance it by making your environment relaxing.

Don't meditate around other people because you will be distracted unless they are meditating too. Use soothing music to help you enter a more relaxed state, and pull out all the tools that help you feel calm such as incense, candles, essential oils, meditation cushion and shawl or blanket.

Perhaps you need to meditate more consistently and for longer periods of time. Okay, let's say you feel like you actually can relax. The next thing you'll need to make sure you're doing is to meditate every day for longer time periods. If you're spending five minutes a day, that's not going to cut it. If you want to take this seriously and really transform your life with the help of your spirit team, make sure you meditate more than you watch TV. Renowned spiritual author Sonia Choquette emphasizes how important it is to work on connecting to the spiritual realm on a daily basis. I know at first you may struggle to stay awake and your mind will bounce around, but using the same meditation music, following the breathing techniques offered in the next chapter to prepare, and setting your meditation, as you will learn to do, will actually give your mind something to do while keeping your body alert.

You probably also need to learn to still the mind while meditating. Once you get to a place where you're consistently meditating every day for at least twenty minutes, you'll probably then start to find your mind cannot focus. The meditations in the subsequent chapters give your mind something to do until you're ready to not use guided meditations. It's best to continue to use these meditations to get used to being in a meditative state and staying focused. Don't jump ahead in the book to the part where you're already working with spirit guides either because you'll miss the part where you build the foundation in your meditation practice that starts to get you used to being in that state. You can't go from zero to sixty when it comes to meeting your spirit guides, so take each step and work on it diligently.

You may need to stop trying to control the message subconsciously. Once you are able to meditate without your mind jumping all over the place, you'll start to have your ego come in. The ego will be discussed further and you will know how to deal with it, but before you do the meditation to move the ego aside, it's important to know some of the ways it blocks you from meeting your guides. The ego is not smart. It can help us keep up with a plan we create. It can help us stay safe. It can help us with basic stuff, but it doesn't have wisdom and isn't aware of itself as we are when we are in a spiritual state. The ego doesn't realize that you as a person can and should evolve, and its mechanism is to try to keep things the way they are. It will come up as confusion, excuses as to why you just shouldn't meditate, or doubt that you can do it. It also may come into your meditation to make you think you're important. When you get messages of self-importance, remember this: anything that promotes self-importance is just the ego being the ego and is not truly helpful.

And ultimately, we all continue to need to address our healing. You may have cleared some energy awhile back but then stopped working on your own healing. If you're going to stay in a high-vibration state and be able to tune into the frequency where your guides can connect to you, you'll also have to be working on healing your energy. This type of healing can come in many forms. You may choose to do daily breathwork to clear the subconscious. You may get Reiki regularly to keep your energy clear. However, this book will teach you a direct healing sequence in chapter 3 ("Meditation to Find the Root Memory" and then "Meditation to Implant a New Memory"). This should become a daily part of your spiritual routine and not just a one-and-done healing meditation.

You Never Have to Take Your Spirit Guide's Advice

This is a really important topic to address before you start working with your guides. Your guides are likely more spiritually evolved because they exist at a higher frequency, but guides also have different frequencies and aren't always able to perceive the perfect advice to offer you. You may get advice from them that feels like something you will do in the future and you may feel it's best not to use their advice right away. You may also just choose to disregard it because it feels like something is going to change and this won't be relevant any longer. Your own intuition is the best indicator for choosing whether or not to take your guides' advice. They are simply advisors for you, trying to help you, but they are not dictators and shouldn't be considered as the absolute decision-makers for your life. Most of the time their advice will be sound, but sometimes, for one reason or another, you may choose to do something different.

You don't need to be afraid that the wrath of the gods will come down on you if you don't take their advice. You too are a spiritual being. Your soul has great wisdom and has been through many lifetimes, perhaps in other galaxies or dimensions. You also have free will and may be tuning into a purpose that your guide really doesn't see as top priority. Some guides will focus on your personal happiness and soul evolution, while others will be more concerned about you contributing to the evolution of our species or saving the planet. One guide might show you an impression of a massage studio, which could indicate you need self-care, while another may show you a stage and a microphone, showing you to use your voice for the people. They are like very wise counselors that give good advice and have your best intentions at heart.

How to Avoid Low-Vibe Spirit Guides

This is another big topic that you need to be aware of before you start working with your guides. Many people that do not understand the spirit world do not know that there are spirits who are just as selfish and dull as some people who are alive. A low-vibration guide will make you feel off. They may come off as shady, hidden, or dark, or they may give you the creeps. Sometimes they will show up looking similar to someone you've seen before in meditation, yet it doesn't feel quite right.

To make sure you're avoiding low-vibe spirit guides, a great habit to get into, which you can use each time you meditate, is to use your intention to simply ask the universe to send you the highest possible guides that only work in the light for the greatest good of all.

How to Set Your Intention for Meditation

Each time you are going to do a meditation to connect with your higher self and your spirit guides, this step will help you actually connect to your desired location within the spirit world. Your intention and being specific about the purpose of your meditation through it, will help your consciousness link with your higher self and through your higher self, your guides. This step should be a normal part of your meditation each time so that you can stay on track with your healing and work only with positive healing energy.

At the beginning of each meditation, use this affirmation to set your intention: "I now ask my higher self to connect with me and guides of the highest possible vibration that work only in the light for the greatest good of all."

You can then verify that these guides are who they say they are, much like an ID check at the airport. If it feels off, do the affirmation again until it feels higher in vibration. Your intuition will get used to this process of ID checking and even find it slightly entertaining. You're more likely to have a fake spirit guide show up if you've been more focused on worldly things like sex, money, and physical possessions. This is just a reflection of the state of your consciousness. Try to relax and put on some meditative music if you are having trouble creating a connection that feels "high vibration." Do the breathing exercise in chapter 3 to help raise your vibration, and you'll find your true higher self will show up.

You Cannot Be Hurt by the Spirit World

One reason people often avoid psychic topics altogether is because they may have heard stories of people being messed with by the spirit world. Many of these scary stories are deeply ingrained in our memory at a young age, especially if we are raised in a church that talks about demons and possession without recognizing there are plenty of spiritual helpers that you can contact. If you find yourself blocked by fear of contacting some unwanted spirit, there is also a simple solution to get over this. You may not be meditating or really diving into this because of this subconscious fear. Luckily, fear is an illusion, and you can deal with even deeply rooted ones.

The spirit world cannot hurt you. They are not in a physical body, so even if they aren't good, spirits cannot hurt or harm you. If anything, they are a nuisance, confused as to where they are and asking for you to get a message to someone or feeding on your good vibes.

How to Get Rid of Unwanted Spirits

If you ever feel a negative energy or presence, you do not need to spend a ton of money to get someone to come in and protect you. You have nothing to be afraid of. You need only to tell them to go away and affirm that only positive energy is allowed around you.

That saying "walk your talk" comes into play here. Because of the law of attraction, if we are harboring anger that we haven't dealt with, we may attract the vibration of anger in the spirit world. We may sense this anger in meditation, which is nothing to be afraid of but merely a helpful indicator that there is something in your subconscious ready to be recognized and released with the meditations in chapter 3 called "Find the Root Memory" and "Implant a New Memory."

If you do the meditations and feel like unwanted spirits haven't gone away, that's when it's okay to ask a trusted spiritual advisor to help you heal your vibration. Sometimes we all need a little help with our healing, even those of us who offer healings full-time. There's nothing to be ashamed of when it comes to asking for help, but I do want to caution you about people who do house clearings. If you ever feel like they are motivating you with fear to get you to spend more money and not helping you heal energy within yourself, they aren't really working with pure intentions.

Fear has been used by people who prey on vulnerable minds who have been indoctrinated into certain spiritual systems that teach there is a lot to fear in the spirit world. If you find someone telling you more and more things to be afraid of, making you feel paranoid and that if you don't buy their cleansing product or use their service, something bad will happen, don't buy into it. Someone working in the light who knows the truth won't need to do this to you.

How to Tell if Your Ego Is Posing as a Spirit Guide

You will get to dive deeper into how the ego can create confusion in your meditations later on, but one way the ego will show up in your meditations is as a fake spirit guide. If your ego really wants something, it may show up as a spirit guide and tell you to do something that feels more like the old you. They may encourage you to do something that would provide instant gratification and feels like it is solely self-serving. While your real spirit guides will help you honor and release guilt about your desires, they will never try to get you off of your soul's path to your highest calling. Your ego would show up as a guide and tell you something like "it's time to go out and party" because it seeks attention and instant pleasure, while a real spirit guide would encourage you to find a group of fun, conscientious people who are going to care for you and not just use you for a good time.

This type of discernment comes over time, but usually if the spirit guide seems to have a bravado or edge to them, they are likely your ego masquerading as a high-vibration guide. You will start to be able to sense the fake guides because it won't feel loving, kind, and safe. The messages that an egoistic guide will give often encourage you to seek fame and fortune, while a real guide will encourage you to be humble and help the world.

The ego can be tricky, which is why we will be spending time working with it later on in the book. But now your mind is prepared to sense when a guide might show up that is trying to get you back into your old ways of living based on your primal instincts. There is nothing wrong with having a good time, but you do need to protect yourself from people who don't care about your well-being. The same goes for guides that show up telling you that you will be super rich very quickly and how to do it. These guides are egoistic projections trying to fill a void in your self-esteem that can only be filled by connecting to your spiritual self and recognizing you don't need to be rich to love yourself and be happy.

Contacting Your Higher Self

*A*s you've been reading this book, you've probably started to get an inkling of the spirit world, but for you it still might seem like a far-off, possibly not even real idea. That's okay. It's like thinking about Bora Bora. It's only an idea we have until we go there. But if we watch a video about it, read a tourism book, and talk to someone who lived there, we can start to get a clearer picture of it before we go. That's where you are now in your journey to meeting your spirit guides. You know they probably exist, but you still may be unsure if you will ever meet them, just as you dream of going to a distant location and wish to one day put your feet in that sand.

If you've ever planned a vacation, one thing that helps besides daydreaming is deciding you are going to go, getting your passport, and packing your bag. You've started to understand the exciting things that await you when you meet your guides in chapter 1 (the practical ways your life will improve), and you've gotten to sense your energy field in chapter 2. Now you may be at the point where you need your passport. Your higher self is like a passport to meet your guides. The passport allows you to travel to another land, and your higher self allows you to travel through other dimensions and meet other beings.

The higher self is the perfect intermediary between you and your spirit guides because the higher self is not limited by the ego and can perceive in a more spiritual way without the barriers of the conditioned mind. Why not just stop once you meet your higher self? Well, the higher self is tied to you and your soul, and while it is the wisest part of you, it may not have the variety of insights available from spirit guides that can help you develop and grow. In other words, while the higher self can nourish you, it's great to have a variety of foods.

In this chapter you will start out by getting into a meditative state. This is an essential preparation for meeting your higher self because it puts you in a relaxed state that will allow your third eye to become the focus of your mental energy. When we are amped up and not relaxed, our thoughts bounce around like Ping-Pong balls in a wind tunnel, but when we do some simple breathing, as you are about to do, you will feel meditation becomes much easier and more vivid.

Developing a relationship with your breath is a huge part of connecting to the spirit world. Your life-force energy enters your body through your breath and is the very means by which you can shift your energy. The breath is often forgotten about in our daily life. However, if you've used deep breathing to calm yourself, you can likely attest that it's powerful. In just a few moments, the breath can offer you the relaxation that people pay for in a weeklong retreat.

To prepare for the breathing exercise, simply sit in a chair with your feet on the ground and your back straight. Place your hands so the palms face up on your thighs in a receiving position.

You may want to record the rest of this section in your own voice, speaking slowly and clearly, leaving room for the amount of breaths it says to take. This will allow you to close your eyes and just listen.

Breathe in your nose for four seconds and breathe out of your nose for four seconds. Continue this cycle and relax deeper on each exhale. Breathe deeper and just relax for a few rounds of breath. Now as you breathe in, envision breathing in golden energy that fills your aura. Each inhale fills your aura, widening it like a balloon. Take a few more deep breaths, expanding your aura.

The high-vibration golden energy is able to push the negative vibrations out of your aura. Now, to really clear the aura and raise your vibration, powerfully breathe in your nose and out of pursed lips six times. Envision pushing all low-vibration energy away from you.

Take a few more calm, slow breaths just sitting in the energy you have created. Notice how it sparkles and there is a sense of excitement in it. Now take one more breath to come back to where you are sitting.

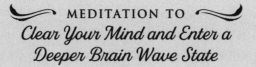

Now that your body is relaxed, this meditation will help you address the mind. Anytime you wish to connect with your guides, you need to be in a more relaxed state than you are when you're going about your day. Your mind basically needs to be blank instead of processing lots of information. These different states are actually measured scientifically by sleep study specialists. The different brain wave states help us understand why we have these experiences through our third eye during meditation but can't snap our figures at any time and get intuitive information as easily.

This meditation will get you calm enough to do the guided meditations in this book. You may want to work with this meditation for a few days or more until you notice a difference in the way you feel. If meditation is a very new thing for you, this will be one of the most valuable tools in this book. It will help you slow your mind, which you likely aren't used to directing in such a bird's-eye-view way.

Congratulations! You are doing something that, in certain times throughout history, only very elite monks and spiritually trained people were able to do. This state of peace you're about to cultivate and learn to reach can help you greatly in managing stress, enhancing creativity, and improving your health. If you notice you start becoming more prolific in some form of art or expression as you go through this book, it's because creativity is activated through relaxation, and ideas show up in the imaginative part of the third eye. It is through your ability to imagine that you will start to see there is a world beyond what you can perceive with your eyes.

Sit in a chair with your feet on the floor. You may want to record the meditation. Try to work on using a calm, soothing voice and do not rush as you read it out loud for the recording.

~

Breathe in your nose and out of your mouth. You are relaxing deeper and deeper. You are letting go of each thought as it enters your mind. There is nothing wrong with having a thought, and it is amazing how you are able to simply set the intention to let it go when it shows up. You are very calm, very peaceful, breathing slowly in and out of your nose.

Notice if your mind takes you down a path, and release that string of thoughts. Allow your body to become heavy as you give yourself permission to let go. Just let your muscles turn to soft melted butter. You are now in a thoughtless, relaxed state. Stay here for a few minutes; just enjoy the space of thoughtlessness as you breathe slowly and deeply.

When you're ready, take three deep breaths to bring yourself back to waking consciousness.

~

Notice how you feel and how at ease you are. You may want to take a break before moving on to the next meditation or you may want to continue. Use your intuition to check in with yourself and see if you need to eat something, go to the bathroom, or just take a break. You don't need to plow through this process as this is going to be helping you change the way you think. Taking on a new habit of meditation happens over time, and being consistent with your meditation each day is more important than quickly getting through this book or chapter. That way, you will develop a long-term relationship with your guides instead of just shooting for an instant connection that may lead to frustration and abandoning your efforts.

I know the tendency to want to do it all right now comes from our productive mindsets, but impatience doesn't serve us in the spirit world. Relax, tune into what your body needs, and even take a nap if that's what you feel like doing.

To this day I still start my meditations by clearing my chakras. This meditation will become automatic for you because it will quickly get you into a meditative state. You want to be honest with yourself about whether you're ready to try the guided meditation. If you're still questioning whether meditation works while trying to meditate or analyzing your success or failure, you probably just are not relaxing deep enough to get past the analytical part of the brain. I'd suggest going back to the breathing and relaxation meditation a few more times until you get that feeling where your thoughts drop for the most part.

It's common to go through periods in your life when meditation is easier and harder. Based on your level of stress, you may find it easy to drop in and visualize or you may suddenly feel blocked. Know that these periods come and go, and when you're having trouble focusing, even after years of meditation, do not be hard on yourself but instead use tools that will help deepen your meditation such as wooden flute music, chakra bowl music, incense, dim lights, and slower, deeper breathing. Also, when you feel like you can't go deep, you're probably skimping on your meditation time. It requires steady, consistent time in meditation to keep that connection strong.

Begin this meditation by sitting in an upright position either cross-legged or in a chair with your feet flat on the floor. Rest your hands gently on your thighs or in your lap with your palms always facing up in a receiving position. You may want to record this meditation in your own voice, speaking calmly and slowly.

Close your eyes and begin to take deep breaths in and out of your nose. Relax as you inhale and exhale three times. Now begin to visualize a vibrant red orb at the base of your spine. As you breathe deeply, it becomes more vibrant and strong. This is your root chakra and the source of your stability and energy. See this red energy pulling up raw life-force energy from the core of the earth.

Now, on your next inhale, bring your attention to the point just below your navel. Visualize an orange orb here. This is the sacral chakra and the source of your creativity, joy, and deep connections with others. As you breathe, see the orange energy glow brighter.

On your next inhale, shift your focus to the upper stomach, right below where your ribs meet. This is your solar plexus chakra, which resonates with the color yellow and is the source of your sense of optimism and confidence. As you breathe, see the orb brighten like the sun.

Now, taking another deep breath, shift your focus to the heart area. Envision the green orb that sits at the chest and expands about a foot around your body. This is your largest chakra, the heart chakra, which is the portal to the upper chakras. This green, glowing orb is allowing you to feel compassion, self-love, and deep empathy for the world. Take a deep breath and see the green become even more vibrant.

With your next inhale, your focus shifts to your throat and you visualize a blue orb here. This is where spirit communicates to you and how you share your truth with the world. Take a deep breath and notice how the blue begins to sparkle.

Now take a deep, slow, powerful breath as you move your focus to the third eye, just above where the eyebrows meet. This is the mystical gateway to the soul. There is a plane of purple (or indigo) light here moving in all directions. This allows you to see beyond time and space. See the purple become deeper as you breathe and charge this chakra.

Bring your focus to the crown of the head, where your crown chakra shimmers and dances, creating a portal between you and the spirit world and beings of light. You see a golden white and pinkish (or violet) light floating from the top of your head upward as high as you can see. As you take two more breaths, the energy becomes so strong that you feel it on the top of your head.

Now visualize the white energy traveling down your spine to the base, where it meets with the red energy. They combine to make a beautiful pink, and the energy fills your aura. Take a deep breath in your nose and out of your mouth, extending your aura as you inhale and exhale three times. Sense all of your chakras as alive and glowing in the house of your aura, which speaks back and forth with them. Slowly open your eyes and return to the room in a relaxed state.

～

If you notice that one chakra seems to be blown out or very small, spend extra time on that chakra; just sending your energy to it can help it come into balance. Each orb will be about the size of an orange or grapefruit except for the heart, which is about the size of a basketball or small exercise ball. As you develop in your spiritual practice, your visualization may shift to see toroidal spheres like a donut and more elaborate energy patterns that interact with your aura. There's no wrong way to do this, so don't overthink it. Just bringing your mind's eye to your energetic system will help you prepare to meet your spirit guides.

MEDITATION TO
Activate the Third Eye

You are starting to get to the really mystical part now! You never know what cool experiences you will start to have as you begin opening to the spirit world. As we discussed, before you meet your spirit guides, you will meet your higher self, but you will never be able to do that if your third eye is blocked. Your third eye often becomes blocked because of calcification of the pineal gland. You may need to change your diet in addition to doing this meditation for a while before moving on to the next meditation. Until you start to see a movie screen when you close your eyes, your third eye is not yet open. By "movie screen" I mean colors, images, and ideas that come to you that you are not trying to create.

Decalcifying the pineal gland through your diet can be done by removing fluoride from your toothpaste and drinking water, eating more raw plants, and eating foods that specifically help alkalize your body such as lemons, greens, and alkaline water. Regular meditation, breathwork, and yoga can help get prana (energy) to your third eye to help activate it. My book *Psychic Yoga* goes over this in greater detail.

However, it's not too soon to start doing this meditation for the third eye. Your third eye is at the brow point, so it would help to record this meditation and be able to focus there with your eyes closed while listening to the meditation. If you have already been recording these meditations, think about whether your own voice may have distracted you or been rushed and try to be more meditative and calm when you record. You can save these recordings to use frequently as you work on your connection to your guides. Developing a real connection to your guides takes time, and you're well on your way to doing it and receiving the infinite healing blessings that await you and those you will help.

～

Sit in a chair with your feet on the floor. If you're not warmed up, do some slow deep breathing to expand your aura before you begin.

It is now time to activate your third eye. This is a momentous occasion and will be a turning point in your life. This is something your soul is cheering you on for doing, and it is the gateway to the spiritual growth you crave. Know that it will give you an unshakable inner strength.

Breathe in and out of your nose slowly, going within your mind's eye and tuning out the external world. Bring your focus to the front of the brain and envision a large eye. This is your third eye. Notice the magnetism of this eye and how it seems to hold secrets and wisdom. Is the eye open or closed when you look at it? If it is closed, ask it to open. This is a very important intention to set because it will open you to the unseen realms. This is a safe journey and a loving step toward your soul's evolution.

Peer into the eye and just observe. Maybe you see a scene before you or perhaps there is a color or a tunnel. Whatever shows up is fine. You may even see something that is blocking you from this process such as a person you live with who has strong judgments about spiritual topics. That still helps you know what you can put aside to continue on your journey. Now that your third eye is opened with the power of your intention, we are going to really focus on this energetic connection. Allow yourself to step into the eye and walk around in this space. Perhaps you notice there are different laws of physics and things float and appear and disappear. This is essentially another realm, an energetic space where you can communicate with the universal grid of consciousness.

Notice as you look around that it continues in all directions. This space is infinite. Spending time here without a goal could be fun, but you could also feel like there is too much to know. For the purpose of meeting your spirit guides, you will visit this space to meet with your higher self, and then you will go on journeys together. You will be able to bring up questions here that will help you utilize this space you are now able to access. Tapping into universal consciousness is a realm with infinite benefits for you, and your higher self will be your guide. It is something that will become more valuable the more you visit and the more you see its power in your life. There is nothing here that can hurt you. It will merely show you things you wish to see, need to see, or would benefit from knowing.

Now take three deep breaths, coming back to the space you're in. Jot down anything that stood out to you in the meditation. If you were unable to visualize this or the eye wouldn't open, just relax and know that you are on your way in perfect time. Focus on the previous exercises until they become second nature before returning to this meditation. It would be good to return to this meditation a few times so that it really feels like you're there and that your third eye is active. You may just sense the shift or actually feel energy at the front of the head throughout the day. Sometimes as the third eye opens, people see flashing light with their eyes closed. It's common to start seeing more synchronicities and connections in daily life as this happens. Your creativity will also start to increase after you work with this meditation.

This is a good time to remind you that this process isn't something that just happens like the flip of a switch. It requires daily practice and significant time with genuine openness to what you may discover. Your own intention to commit to the process is essential in the mission to meet your spirit guides. Just as you wouldn't get a degree in college without trying, you must follow the process and sign up to meet these guides.

MEDITATION TO
Meet Your Higher Self

It is now time to meet the messenger that will work between you and your guides. Your higher self is the part of you that exists beyond the ego in this lifetime. This is the spiritual part of you that is much wiser than your egoistic mind. It knows beyond time and space and sees your own identity from a spiritual perspective, where your actions are measured by love and connection to the greater good. This part of you helps you see what is in your best interests and what is just an illusion created by the idea that you must compete to be happy. This part of you also acts as your guide within the spirit realms to help you connect to high-vibration-loving spirit guides. Your higher self is the guide that has been there all along in your heart or in the back of your head, trying to help you avoid making bad decisions or helping you know someone's true intentions.

In this meditation you will meet your higher self and get to know what it is like to commune with this part of you. This will be a wonderful experience, and you might feel like your favorite person is visiting you even though it is your first time officially meeting in this lifetime. You may have asked your higher self for help or guidance before, not knowing who you were addressing. In the process of understanding how to work with the spirit world and how your identity fits within it, this step is going to unlock a lot for you. The mind perceives the world in linear time, and your higher self can navigate between realms and times. Your higher self is like a best friend with superpowers. This is the most important relationship you can cultivate in your lifetime, and this spiritual part of you is within your soul. This part of you is very easy to talk to and will always be there when you need wisdom.

~

Start by taking slow deep breaths in and out of your nose. Relax as you begin to go within yourself and the external world becomes very quiet. You are about to enter into the four-dimensional space-time continuum, which is beyond the physical realm of earth. The fourth and fifth dimensions are the next highest realms of consciousness, where you will now begin to work in your process of meeting your spirit guides. You have seen this realm in your third eye activation meditation, and now it's time to see what you will do in this realm. Your higher self sits in the fourth dimension but can also communicate with the higher dimensions (which go up to twelve, according to very advanced channelers). Many of your spirit guides exist in the higher realms.

Jesus Christ was said to be a ninth-dimensional being, and your own soul may have memories of lifetimes in some of these other dimensions. You may notice that not everything has a permanent gender or physical form here, as energy has a purpose and moves by that purpose. The energetic imprint of your higher self will match your subconscious and be projected to you in a way that will help you connect at that time. Your higher self may make you smile by showing up as Elvis or they may just show up as a space like a desert. It can be abstract, but the feeling of your higher self will begin to be familiar enough that you'll know the feeling of connecting with them even when there is a change of appearance.

Bring your focus to the mind's eye and envision yourself in space, up above the earth, above all that you know and that is familiar. You are floating, free from gravity, and feeling very comfortable. It is the perfect temperature and you can travel around using your intention. Find a space far enough away from earth where you're no longer thinking about your life there but more interested in the energy that you're encountering in this vast and curious space that seems to be alive.

Your higher self will now come toward you. Your higher self is much larger than your body and can seem gigantic to you. Your higher self is pure love, and the entire reason for your higher self's existence is to help you heal and make good decisions in this lifetime. Just as your soul chose to be in this lifetime, your higher self is a part of that decision to take this journey with you. You will feel a deep sense of kindness and familiarity with your higher self and just enjoy being close. There is unquestionable loyalty, trust, and dedication felt instantly.

Your higher self will now sit across from you at a table. As you sit here feeling the love, your chakras connect one at a time. The root chakra connects at the base of the spine. The sacral chakra connects at the navel. The solar plexus connects at the upper stomach. The heart chakra connects at the chest. The throat chakra connects. The third eye chakra connects. The crown chakra connects. As you look into your higher self's eyes, you're already receiving an energetic transmission that is shifting your mind's energy to be more in line with your spiritual identity, your soul purpose. This is going to help you shed the harmful patterns that originate in your own addiction to being just a human without a bigger spiritual purpose. You don't need to do anything—there is no work to accomplish, just this connection.

Feel the love and care that is here for you and how real it is. Your heart chakra connection is a way to receive messages, and looking into your higher self's eyes is as well. Often you may be guided to follow your higher self in meditations, but you can also use this table to sit and ask your higher self questions as you work with your guides.

Your higher self is a great translator, and you will only be able to work with your guides as you merge with this spiritual part of yourself more. This is going to be a joyful relationship with total commitment and no fear. Your higher self is going to show you how to find peace with your life and the things you experience. Your higher self has great gifts for you and will open you to great power with the ability to forge relationships with multidimensional beings whose wisdom lies beyond the constructs of planet Earth in the year that you currently breathe, eat, and exist.

Thank your higher self for meeting you and know you can return at any point. You may take three deep breaths to bring yourself back to the space you're seated in.

Jot down what it was like to meet your higher self and if you noticed anything resisting this process. Often our ego will throw a distraction into our meditation to stop our change process. The growth you're going to experience scares the ego because it isn't smart, to put it bluntly. It just wants your body to survive and works to block foreign thoughts. If you had a distraction (like a dancing monkey) in your visualization, next time you'll know to name it so that it doesn't pull your focus.

There is no right or wrong in this; just observe and see how it helps you note where your own ego comes into your meditation. The ego can pop up in different ways to block your spiritual process, and when it does, try not to react with a big emotional response; just note it as if you're taking notes while watching a video and you'll train yourself to bypass it.

Your ego will sometimes make it seem like you're too busy to meditate or give you a physical symptom that makes it seem like you just can't do it. Remember the ego only knows how to keep your physical body alive and resists all new things even if they are good for you. The resistance is the way when it comes to spiritual growth. If the resistance is really strong and you really don't feel up to meditation, just relax and use the time to keep your vibration high by taking care of yourself. There's no need to force your meditations as the process amplifies when you're joyful. So getting in touch with what brings you joy will help you know how much time to put into meditation and avoid spiritual burnout.

This meditation is going to help you recognize how the ego shows up in meditations and give you a specific way to bypass the ego before it starts to pop in. Doing this simple intention-setting visualization at the beginning of all your meditations will become automated because it is so very helpful and it will shift your energy to be able to tune out the mind's worries and tune into the spirits' fun messages.

Sit up tall and begin breathing slowly and deeply through your nose. Relax as you exhale, feeling yourself sinking into the place you're sitting. Begin to go within yourself as the outside world fades away. You will now return to outer space, where you met your higher self, and waiting with your higher self will be a duplicate of them but with different energy. This is your ego, which acts like your higher self sometimes but doesn't have the same energetic imprint and can't possibly compare to the amazing feelings your higher self offers. The duplicate feels self-serving and looks for instant pleasure. It wants things that are going to give them adrenaline, and it would probably advise you to seek them too. That is why you must give them a task and a place to be in while you're in meditation. In this space, give them a mansion with everything they could ever want—then lock them in the mansion with all of their happy things. This will keep your ego out of your meditation and keep the thoughts they often try to interject from coming in so much.

Putting your ego in the mansion so they are happy will help you work more easily and efficiently with your higher self. If you feel like your ego keeps coming into your meditation, you can always just envision putting them back in the mansion with their favorite things such as foods, indulgences, and earthly things that they think are the source of happiness. Your higher self and you have important work to do that will bring much deeper satisfaction, and the not-so-smart ego will happily stay in that mansion while you do it.

If your higher self shows up but doesn't feel right, know that is your ego. Affirm that they must go and request your higher self show up. This is common for a while until we get used to trusting our higher self, so it's very helpful to use the mansion at the beginning of the meditation just like you get into a meditative state by clearing your chakras.

Now that it's just you and your higher self, they will lead you to the mansion of your soul, where you will learn how to clear your own energy. This is where you will get to clear the low vibrations that are making it seem like bad things happen to you. This is also where you will get to clear the heavy, dense energy that creates emotional pressure, which feels like stress and anxiety. As you raise your vibration using the mansion of your soul with your higher self, you will raise your vibration high enough to meet your guides. This process is simple, inspiring, and exciting!

Your own life will start to shift as you work in the mansion of your soul. See the mansion in the distance and approach with your higher self. Walk up the steps and stand at the front door. Your higher self takes your hand and together you walk into this energetic mansion, which holds much wisdom about you and who you are. You will use this space in the next meditation, but for now just look around and observe the space and how it reflects the loving qualities within you. This place is going to become familiar and feel familiar very soon. For now, you have done great work and can exit with your higher self. Thank your higher self.

Knowing you can return at any point, take three deep breaths to bring yourself back to where you are.

⌒

Jot down anything you noticed in the meditation and how you felt by dealing with the ego. Notice if your ability to visualize is getting stronger and how different it feels meditating now than when you first started.

How to Clear Your Own Low Vibrations So You Can Meet Your Spirit Guides

Just as it is very hard to reach flying speeds without jet fuel, it is very hard to connect to your guides without high-octane vibrations. If you're feeling really angry, your consciousness is sitting in a state of angst and disharmony that blocks the connection. The source of our emotional state is in our subconscious mind. This journey of meeting your spirit guides is one that requires you to give yourself high-octane emotions so your vibration will reach higher altitudes.

The good news is, this is simple and anybody can do it. All it takes is some good guided meditation, some reflection, and processing. All of this is what you are about to do. This is a very similar process to what you would do in psychotherapy but is more geared toward connecting you to the spiritual advisors that will help you see how and why you operate the way you do from an even deeper layer. While psychology itself is a very helpful practice, it doesn't lead to a spiritual relationship with your soul, which will allow you to go within to answer questions. This type of strength is invaluable in life because you will stop comparing yourself to the standards others have for you and themselves and start realizing your true purpose.

The following two meditations are ones you can do indefinitely because this healing process has many, many layers that can go back even to prior lifetimes and into your ancestral memories. Today we will keep it simple and start with whatever spirit shows you is most important. This reveals the beliefs you accept as truths that are hurting you. The process basically involves seeing a belief you hold as absolute truth and then seeing where the belief came from.

Let's just give an example so you see what I mean. A girl raised in a very science-minded household by atheist parents who made fun of spirituality may have adapted the same attitude without realizing it. She accepts that we are finite, controlled by the process of life and death, and that we must create our own opportunities. She doesn't believe in the spirit world and doesn't take anyone who does seriously. However, she also pushes herself so hard that she doesn't enjoy her life. Her desire to find meaning in her life has overrun her emotionally, and her core understanding of life has jeopardized her ability to feel good. In the meditation she may see her parents talking about science or putting down anything related to energy or emotional intelligence. This realization might encourage her to explore the science-backed studies of the spiritual realms and understand her parents' viewpoints and how it shaped her own worldviews.

This one simple meditation might lead, over time, to a softening of her own worldview to leave room for spirituality without leaving her love for science. This could also allow her to find deeper meaning in things besides facts and accomplishments that would bring great peace to her and improve her overall health by lowering her stress. This is an example of a practical way in which the following meditation could prove to raise her emotional state, thus giving her a high-octane frequency capable of accessing different dimensions.

Seeing Reflections and Patterns

This abstract type of meditation often reveals itself through a pain point or a series of pain points in our life. We may see a charged memory that has been bothering us and is essentially keeping us in a very aggravated state. It may be a tiff we had with a sibling or an insult received by a stranger. Whatever the pain point is, you will be able to use it to discover how it links back to helping you raise your frequency.

This can free you from a lot of pain and heartache that may be your baseline emotional state. Just to give another quick example, let's say a man is discontent with his job because he feels he is undervalued, underpaid, and unchallenged. His ego tells him he is failing in life, and he tries to bury this emotion by diving into relationships that give him excitement. However, he doesn't see that his parents have always told him being a man means making money and supporting a woman. Because he hasn't lived up to his parents' ideal, he feels like a failure. He rushes his relationships and doesn't realize he is getting into relationships for the wrong reasons. This pattern leaves him feeling out of control, unhappy, and like he is destined to be alone.

If he was able to see this pain point's root cause, he could see that just being nice to the people already in his life would make things more enjoyable. He would see that his self-worth is about how kind he is and not how much is in his bank account. This could transform his worldview to allow his emotional state to raise and also allow him to start to perceive higher realms of consciousness.

You do not need to uncover all your beliefs in one meditation session—that would take way too long. Just do one or two in your meditation and stick to the meditation daily or at least once a week. Definitely use the meditations when something feels off or bothers you because they will help you shift your energy.

Start sitting up straight and keep your feet flat on the floor. Make sure you're comfortable, relaxed, and excited to do this.

Begin to breathe slowly and deeply in and out of your nose. Relax deeper and deeper on each exhale. Begin to go within yourself, letting the outside world fade away. You will meet your higher self in outer space.

As your higher self approaches, feel the familiar feeling and the love emanating from the heart. Take a moment to put the ego in its mansion so it will not interfere with your meditation. All the things that the ego desires go with it.

Your higher self will lead you to your soul mansion, where you will visit the indoor movie theater of your life memories. Give yourself anything you would like in this space to feel comfortable. You might like a big comfy chair and your favorite candy.

Sit down and ask your higher self this:

Show me the most important experience that has created a belief, attitude, or pattern of action that doesn't align with my soul.

You will see a memory, and it may surprise you or seem minor, but it is important nonetheless. Once you see a memory, ask your higher self how it is giving you a negative perspective and how it's affecting your energy. Write this down in your journal.

~

You will return to this space to do the healing work, but for now take a deep breath and bring yourself back to the space you are sitting to write freely about how this memory is linked to your worldview, attitude, or actions. When you feel like you've flushed out your thoughts, continue to the next meditation.

If no memory showed up, it may be that your mind needs to take care of something so you can relax fully. Sometimes when we aren't fully present, we may feel that blank feeling and sometimes we are afraid to see a memory. Try to relax more and know you're in a safe place if this is happening. If you don't see a memory, just wait and breathe. If one doesn't come after a few minutes, try the meditation again when you feel your energy is more calm.

Now you will heal this pattern and be able to relinquish the sting of this pain point. Remember, you will have a higher vibration once you are free from this energetic pattern, and you will be able to meet your spirit guides and work with them on your soul purpose. Healing the energy is not hard; it will simply allow your subconsciousness to shift and allow you to create a new energetic pattern.

Breathe slowly and deeply. You are on the great journey with your higher self to meet your spiritual guides and are very near that moment. When you're working with them, you'll realize just how much you were transforming in this very moment. Congratulate yourself for making it to this point. Many do not have the privilege to get to this level of awareness in their lifetime, and you're awakening spiritually in this very moment, empowering yourself over fear.

Meet your higher self outside your soul mansion and walk in together hand in hand, ready to heal and transform your energy. Find a comfortable seat in your life movie theater and return to the memory that you found. Knowing this is creating a negative energetic loop, ask your higher self this:

What alternative event would create a positive belief and shift this pattern to an empowering, soul-aligned energy?

Since the past is now just energy, you are moving energy as you do this. This harmless work will simply heal your energy and free you of the past. As your higher self reveals an alternate event, watch this more loving, healing event and see how you feel. Take a deep breath and write down how you feel about this new energetic awareness and how this event now shapes your attitudes, beliefs, and patterns of behavior that help you align with your soul purpose.

～

Now would be a great time to take a break. Processing energy like this can take it out of you. Have a nourishing meal, a nap, do something that makes you laugh, take a bath—whatever you feel drawn to do. Remember this is all to help you live better in your body, in your real life, and trying to rush the process is neither necessary nor helpful. This is not about escaping your life or ascending out of your body but finding you really want to wake up and meet the world more and more each day. This process is not about the ultimate destination but more about the gentle unfolding of your true self to the world and the development of your awareness within the world to navigate as a spiritual being.

As I am writing this, I keep thinking that if I picked up this book, I'd want to meet my spirit guide on page 1, but this is the process—and it will work, but it does take time. I started to think of the journey as the great journey and that going through the meditations in this book should just be joyful, honorable, and exciting in each part. You do not need to feel like you will get to the good part because you're in it right now.

The resistance or the urge to want it all right now, to arrive, is exactly what you need to recognize at this moment. Accepting you're always right where you need to be will help you enjoy this great journey that is already transforming your experience of your life.

Since you are learning quite a few meditations, you may want to give yourself a structure for your meditation practice. It can be a loose structure if you're not a planner. A good average amount of daily meditation at this point would be about thirty minutes at least so that you can really relax and reflect.

4

Starting to Work with Spirit Guides

*Y*ou have patiently followed the steps to get yourself ready for this. You could not have skipped to this part unless you were already aware of the chakras and had already been working with them. If you are now feeling excited anticipation for what lies ahead, your body is telling you that you are ready. If you feel something is off and that you're jumping ahead, you probably are. Check in with how you feel right now. Do you feel a sense of ease or do you feel like you may be pushing forward because of a tendency to rush? Listen to your own truth.

This is a good process to start to ask yourself because while we like to rush our work in the world so we can hurry up and get to the fun part, in working with spirit, it's only fun when we *don't* rush—when we allow ourselves to have the experiences we are meant to have, feel the feelings that need to be felt, and let things happen instead of force them to happen. This work with spirit is about self-honesty, not speed. Getting the real happiness this work can offer you hinges upon understanding this differentiation between how we approach many things in life and how to approach energetic transformation.

The Way Spirit Guides Show Up

Because guides are nonphysical and may never have been in human form, they can show up in surprising ways with or without gender or as groups, feelings, colors, or other creative expressions that allow your mind to link with them.

Many people experience signs in their dreams and their waking lives that come from the spirit world. These are both ways that your guides send you messages. You may see repeating number sequences or get a song stuck in your head; a message on a billboard or truck may stand out that answers a question on your mind or you may get a visit from a specific animal in a dream. All of these are messages sent from the spiritual realm to help you wake up to a deeper truth that will help you.

From this point on, if you're not already, it will be crucial to keep a daily journal to see patterns that show up between your dreams, your waking life, and your meditations. You may receive a message in meditation that isn't completely clear until something unfolds in your life or you may see something in a dream that will help unlock the meaning of an image you see in meditation.

Spirit guides often communicate with nature or images of nature because they are helping us connect to and come back to who we are and let go of the many burdens we allow in our mind based on societal conditioning. The simplicity of nature and the qualities revealed in the signs we receive are personal to us, and while looking up the meaning of a symbol may help unlock the meaning it has for you, your intuition will guide you to the best interpretation of it. This also helps you get used to accepting subtle truths and not absolutes.

The feelings you get from something can be the message itself. Not having a clear message right away helps you get used to ambiguity and accept that you can have peace without having all the answers. Often a bug or an animal or a natural phenomenon like rain or a river shows up and stands out to us because the spirit world wants us to wake up to a greater truth. They pull our attention to this because it will help us see we need to meditate to alleviate some type of mental or emotional energy we are unconsciously harboring that is causing us pain.

Having Multiple Spirit Guides

You may start with one guide and as you develop, you may meet more guides and be able to contact higher-vibrational guides. Understanding vibrational states helps you see how your relationships with multiple guides may be lifelong or just temporary. You do not need to try to force a guide to stay with you because as your consciousness evolves, so will your relationships in the spirit world. Just be the observer to what and who shows up without trying to control it. This act of observing helps you get into an intuitive and receptive state to read the energy of group consciousness and understand how and why people do things that are not actually good for them. It empowers you to think independently and more critically about your life choices instead of following the crowd, who often are not consciously choosing their lifestyle.

You may find that you have multiple guides because they serve completely different purposes. For years I have had one guide who only gives me the name of herbs at specific moments when I need them and never says anything else. However, she always shows up looking the same and in the same top-left corner in my mind. Other guides I had for years stopped showing up, and eventually my memory of some of them faded as my life evolved and I needed guides with other types of energy.

Just to give you an example of how many you may have at once, at the time I am writing this book, I have two guides I work with on a weekly basis as well as three more that I consult frequently. Occasionally I will have a guest appearance from the consciousness of other spirits, and I still work with the herbal remedy guide. Two of my guides have revealed names to me; the rest of my regulars have not. I do not spend time trying to uncover every detail about their existence but put on my observing and listening hat to see what they would like me to see or know. Instead of trying to control our relationship, I trust that they will tell me the important things.

Working with these guides has helped me to see things in my life on a much deeper level. I have started to understand my own deeper motivations, where I let myself become negative about not being at a certain place in my life, and how to find peace with where I am. Their presence in my life has become an anchor during a time of great uncertainty in the world and during a time when I have been living in severe chronic pain with very few ways to support myself. I bring this up only to offer you a beacon of hope that no matter what you're going through, this relationship you build with the spirit world will allow you to meet who you need, when you need them. The saying "When the student is ready, the teacher will appear" also applies to the spirit world.

MEDITATION TO
Contact Your Spirit Guides

Now it's time to contact your guides! Be patient as you come up against your own resistance or inability to focus. You may feel resistance to the need to meditate more frequently. Based on what we have discussed up to this point, you can expect all of that to come up, so just know that you're right on track. The resistance is the ego grieving its comfort zone. You are shedding layers of yourself that represent when you just thought of the day-to-day things and not of your soul purpose. This is taking you beyond the petty attachments to what people think about you so that their opinions no longer dictate your happiness. This is taking you beyond, to the world of many dimensions where your spirit can intermingle with higher-vibrational beings who consistently stay in a state of peace and love and can guide you to do the same.

This meditation would be good to record and listen to so you can fully relax. Prepare for the meditation as if you are preparing for a distinguished guest to arrive such as an ambassador or a diplomat who is highly regarded by you. Make this moment momentous in that it is the start of something more valuable than your college experience; it is a graduation from lower planes of existence. Whatever happens or doesn't happen in your meditation is perfect today. If you have anxiety, feel really connected, or just follow along without anything epic happening, it is all perfect because what is most important is the momentum you're building in your third eye connection and ability to communicate psychically with the unseen realms. Have your journal handy so you can write after the meditation.

Sit tall with your spine straight and your feet on the ground. You can also sit in a cross-legged position if it's comfortable. Close your eyes and start to focus on your breath. Notice the breath enter your lungs, expanding them on all sides, and notice how your chest falls when you exhale. Follow the energy of the breath as it comes in and exits out of your body. This life-force energy is keeping you alive and has kept you alive your entire life. It keeps the lights on, so to speak, and is electric currents of energy upon which consciousness rides. Following this energy up and out of your body, meet your higher self in space.

Ask your higher self to allow you to meet a high-vibration spirit guide that only works in the light for the highest good for all. This will allow you to meet the highest possible guide you can communicate with at this point.

Your higher self will now take you somewhere. Your higher self remains at the edge of this place so you can journey on and meet your spirit guides. Your higher self will wait for you to return.

As you walk forward, you can glance back and see the happiness and joy in your higher self's eyes that you are taking this step. Come to a space that has a very high vibration and see that in front of you is your spirit guide. Just observe what stands out without judgment and without expectation. Ask the spirit guide if they are of the light and working for the highest good of all. If there is hesitation, do not despair as your ego may be interfering. Ask your ego to kindly go wait in their mansion and request that your true spirit guide be revealed to you now.

You will likely be surprised at what you meet here. Remember a spirit guide does not have to have a human form or any form at all. Guides are a consciousness, an energy of love and wisdom. Continue to breathe as you commune with your spirit guide, taking it all in and feeling their vibration. You have come a great way to meet them and done lots of preparation, and they are just as happy to see you as you are to see them. This is the beginning of an important healing relationship, a fun relationship, and one that will redefine how you wish to be treated in life and what you consider a friend to be. It will help you be a better friend and a wiser person. Knowing you will return to see them soon, say goodbye for now and return to your higher self.

As you and your higher self walk side by side, sense the excitement of this journey you are on together. There is so much yet to happen, but you sense that your higher self knows you were destined to be in this moment together and they smile as you thank them, knowing you can come back to them at any point.

Take a deep breath and return to the space you are in. Give yourself a moment to calibrate to your body and then write down what it was like to meet your spirit guide even if you feel you had difficulty doing so. Take a break by getting up and walking around or just having some tea or a small snack. It's important to take breaks as you do these meditations, knowing your energy is going through changes. Eating some healthy snacks and staying hydrated can help you adjust to these changes.

This meditation is going to help you get to know your guide and why they are in your life. Perhaps you had more than one show up and that is fine. Just work with one and then the other in meditation. Some guides represent a group and will present not as an individual but will feel like you're speaking to a species or a council of elders. They may address themselves as "we," which is something many channelers notice.

This is an exciting step in your journey and even if you don't get an extremely clear answer when you ask them why they are in your life, as you continue to work with them, it will be revealed. Often we look for answers that are about money, love, or personal advancement, but the things that they help us with are of the soul. They are able to help us with concepts we are not yet familiar with that will present themselves as we work with them. For now you will get to know their essence and start to unpack the way they will communicate with you and the type of feelings you get while communicating with them, which is often the message itself.

Again, you may choose to record this meditation or just read from the book. There's no right or wrong, and you can do what feels best.

Sit tall with your feet on the ground and begin to breathe deeply and slowly in and out of your nose. Relax deeper and deeper on each exhale. Begin to go within yourself as the external world fades. Your higher self will meet you and again take you to the place where you met your spirit guide. Your higher self waits for you and is allowing you to get to know your spirit guide. As you approach your spirit guide, see if you notice anything different than you did the first time.

You may simply ask them what they are here to help you with in your life. The answer may not come in the form of a sentence or words but perhaps as an image or a series of images. It may come as a feeling, a color, or a sense of something that you have yet to understand fully. The way they communicate with you may be nonverbal. They may show you an object or something that helps you understand. You will only be able to perceive what your consciousness is ready to perceive, and if right now that is just a good feeling that they are here to help you, that is enough. Their behavior or movement may reveal the quality that they will help imbue your life with or the color you see may help you see the energy they will help you heal as it relates to your chakras.

Write down anything you observe, even if it doesn't make sense. Sometimes you will see something and later in the day it will just click. Your guides like to leave clues for you to make life fun and magical! They are not intentionally obscure, but the way we communicate between realms is energetic, and the more you do it, the easier it is to understand that not all communication is verbal. You can always ask for clarification when they show you something, too.

Thank your guide for now and return to your higher self. You're creating a place in the multidimensional space together with your guide that you will be able to return to daily to meet with them and just allow them to show you what you need to see. Your higher self will always be there with you as your guide. Walk back with your higher self, feeling the bond that you are creating with them and the trust that has already developed.

Allow yourself to thank them. Knowing you can return at any time, take a deep breath and return to where you are.

~

Jot down anything else that comes to mind or that you would like to remember. If you don't have anything to write down now, remember that you're learning and it will come with time. This type of thinking may be very new and just know that each time you try, you're building that momentum. Smile and carry on!

Don't be surprised if you meet a different guide sometimes. There is nothing wrong with that, and keeping an open mind and a pure intention will lead you where you need to be in the spiritual realms.

Sometimes the way your higher self shows up will change; however, your guides, if they follow the same pattern they have for me, will remain pretty much the same or reveal more of themselves to you. While the shapeshifting higher self often morphs, you can expect that your guide's energy will remain relatively constant. This is because your guide is separate from your soul, while your higher self reflects what you need based on your own consciousness. I once had a guide not show up for years and return with the same energy so that I was quickly able to recognize him and remember why he had come into my life before.

If at this point you feel confused, frustrated, or even like giving up, that would be normal. If you're finding yourself trying to talk yourself out of this process, that too would be normal. You are breaking habits, creating new ways of thinking, and challenging what you know! You will have experiences that defy your rational thinking and reveal that the spirit world exists, and if you haven't yet had any experiences like this, that's okay.

One way I first knew that the spirit world existed was by getting accurate readings by psychics. I was blown away that they had all these details about my life and could accurately depict what was in my heart. If you're having doubts, I would recommend getting a reading from someone who gives you a good feeling and not someone who feels like a scammer or like they are trying to get you to spend money by scaring you. The feeling you get when you tune into a healer's energy can help you know whether or not they are evolved enough in their own consciousness to relay information that is both psychic and valuable to you.

Creating an Altar to Help Connect to Your Spirit Guides

Whether you just want to really emphasize and cultivate the relationship with your guides to improve your connection or you're looking for a way to get that relationship to start, creating an altar can help you harness your own energy and direct it to do just that. Altars are a dedicated space for meditation with tools that help you relax and connect to the spirit world as well as have a clear intention. We are so used to focusing on things we can see and touch, people we know, plans we are making, and things that have happened that pulling our focus onto something new to our thought patterns can certainly use all the help we can give it.

Since we are mostly on our phones engaging with people, our attention span is also short, bouncing around every few seconds. In meditation we are practicing keeping our attention, all of our thoughts, in one place for an extended period of time. An altar helps you send a message to your brain that this is important and overrides the little distracting thoughts that might pop in when you're meditating. It is also an opportunity to engage your senses and utilize the very powerful tool of sense memory.

The reason altars often combine things with strong smells like resins, incense, oils, or flowers is because it is our strongest recall sense. To get us into meditation quicker, we can use the same scent to remind us of our past journeys and state of mind. Altars also often include an intention that we can read, pictures of spiritual beings or teachers, as well as items from nature that conjure a feeling of peace. Anything that helps you feel meditative can be included on your altar.

Your dedicated meditation space can include crystals that you feel a sense of upliftment from. Crystals have a high vibration and can help us elevate our frequency to match that of our guide to foster a stronger connection. You do not need to go out and spend a lot of money making an altar, but feel free to splurge if you can because meditating in front of a carefully curated energetic space will help you consistently reach a high-vibration emotional state. Even if you have nothing that looks like your guide, having anything that brings positive emotions to you can help you tune into those frequencies of higher dimensions. This is like a spirit hack as opposed to a life hack.

Refer to the appendix of meditation tools to help you choose tools such as incense, crystals, and oils you would like to include in this sacred space.

This is an exciting next step in your relationship with your spirit guides. If you're already working with multiple guides, you can pose the question in the meditation to them and see who answers. We have gone over how it is important for you to not pigeonhole your interaction by asking narrow questions. Often the best question to ask is simply this: "What do I need to know for my spiritual growth right now?" This type of open-ended question is what I was taught to use, and it is what I have been using for years. It is fun because I will often simply be shown something that I later encounter, and it reminds me that spirit is real!

You can record this meditation or read it if that works for you.

Find a comfortable place to sit and begin to breathe slowly and deeply in and out of your nose. Go ahead and consciously release any specific expectations of how this question will go.

Now meet your higher self and continue to breathe slowly as you relax and walk together to the place where you will ask your guides for the first piece of wisdom in this journey with them. Relax as you approach, breathe, and relax.

Your higher self will wait for you, and you can now commune with your spirit guides. Allow yourself to really just be present with your guides and tune into their energy. Feel the love and wisdom that is their frequency. With an open heart, pose the question that you would like to know what you need to help you on your spiritual path right now. Just observe and wait. You may get something that comes to mind, they may lead you somewhere to show you something, or you may get a message.

If it's unclear, ask for clarification. Breathe and relax. Wait and give yourself time to observe, then write down anything you've observed, even if it's not quite clear yet what the meaning is. Ask them if there is anything else right now you need to know, and wait. Just breathe and patiently relax. If anything comes up, write down anything else they seem to reveal to you. Thank them. Knowing you'll be back soon to work with them, return to your higher self and walk back away from the meeting place.

Take a deep breath, slowly bringing yourself back to your body and writing down anything else you would like to remember or that stood out for you.

~

It's okay if you didn't get a clear message. Just creating a routine of asking is the place to start. You're right where you need to be. Do not get discouraged. Later in the book there are tips that will help you know what to do if you still end up having trouble with these meditations. The whole journey is fun, even any parts where you feel blocked.

CADUCEUS

FLOWER OF LIFE

OM

EYE OF HORUS

ANKH

WHEEL OF LIFE

TRIPLE GODDESS

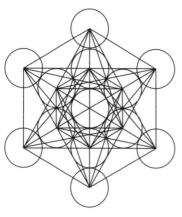

METATRON'S CUBE

CELTIC KNOT

Using Symbols to Connect to Your Spirit Guides

Sacred symbols can help you connect to higher dimensions and alternate realities. Symbols can help unlock parts of your consciousness and past lives and tune you into a certain stream of consciousness. Many people have meditated on and connected to these symbols for ages, which has built a group consciousness that helps you. Think of how you get amped up when you're in a crowd and you can understand how group consciousness can help you raise your frequency. If it's a crowd sitting in meditation, it will help you get into a calm state. If it's a passionate protest march, you will get swept up in the energy as well.

Group consciousness works in other ways, too. Think about how we all feel extra energy on a full moon and how we are all known to be extra anxious on certain days depending on the placements of the planets. Our emotional state is affected by energy outside of ourselves. In this light, using symbols is very similar to the practice of using an ancient mantra or praying to a saint; the many people who have poured their focus on this symbol have created a map that your consciousness can follow. You can often feel that vibration when you enter a very old, spiritual building.

Using symbols allows you to tune into your intuitive and creative side where you can access your third eye and perceive through feelings, images, and subtle knowing. You can read through the history of the symbols, look at them, and see if one in particular calls to you to meditate on. We are often drawn to symbols because our intuition knows it is the frequency of that symbol that can help us with where we are on our path.

It makes sense that spiritual people wear symbols because it helps them connect to spiritual realms of consciousness.

First set the intention to find a symbol that will help you connect to your spirit guide. When you find a symbol you like, just focus on it by looking at it or seeing it in your mind's eye, then see where your mind goes. These symbols are popular sacred symbols that are linked to positive energy and meaning. You may also find a symbol not listed that helps you raise your vibration and connect intuitively to the higher realms.

ANKH: Also called the Key of Life, this Egyptian symbol reminded wearers that life is only a part of the eternal journey of the soul. The symbol is a hieroglyph meaning "breath of life" that stood for both life in the body and in the afterlife. It was likely the inspiration for the cross in Christianity, which represents eternal life offered by Jesus. It is also said to be the belt buckle of the goddess Isis, representing fertility and light.

CADUCEUS: Also known as the Staff of Hermes, this symbol is a wand entwined by two snakes. This ancient occult symbol is not just the symbol of modern medicine, it also represents the balance of the mystical trifecta of divinity portrayed in many cultures. One interpretation is that the snakes are the yin and yang energies in our body, which when balanced allow for enlightenment. It reminds us that the masculine and feminine energies in each of us, when balanced, allow the kundalini to rise so we can experience superconsciousness. In this interpretation,

the wand is the spine of the human body, with the
wings being the expanding mind.

CELTIC KNOT: The symbol of one unending strip that
winds, weaves, and loops around itself represents
the unending cycle of life. It brings to mind the
interconnection and dependence between the physical
and spiritual aspects of being. The symbol is most
commonly associated with Celtic culture but can be
traced to before the Roman era to the Byzantines.
The symbol is given many meanings, including that of
eternal love, making it often a gift of romantic gesture.

EYE OF HORUS: An Egyptian symbol of protection
and healing, the eye of Horus was said to have been
magically restored after a series of battles when Horus
sought to avenge his father's death. People use amulets
of this symbol to connect to healing energy and ward
off energy that is unwanted. There is also a hidden
Fibonacci sequence (known as the golden spiral, with
perfect mathematical proportions) within the eye,
which reveals the universe operates by a higher order
of laws that connects us all to a harmonious web of
support.

FLOWER OF LIFE: This symbol represents the energy
that connects all of us beyond time and space.
It is considered sacred geometry and consists of
overlapping circles that create perfect harmony and
symmetry that can be found in our bodies, in nature,
and even in different observations of energy-like
sound waves. It is said that this energy holds the

Akashic record of all of life and helps expand the heart to sense through compassion. Interestingly, this symbol has been discovered in many different cultures throughout the world.

METATRON'S CUBE: The balance of this symbol as well as the structure of it is meant to represent the similar patterns that reveal a unifying energy that is the very essence of all creation. The symbol links to archangel Metatron, who is said to oversee the energy that connects all living things and the very building blocks of DNA. It correlates to the tree of life and the crown chakra, through which we can find our spiritual connection.

OM: This symbol represents the essence of reality or consciousness, which is the creative sound of the universe. It comes from Indian religions and is a Sanskrit symbol. The curves represent the different states of mind to remind us the mind often creates the illusion that we are not connected, but by using the sound of OM, or *aum*, we can connect to the creative energy of the universe and reach transcended consciousness.

TRIPLE GODDESS: Also known as the Triple Moon symbol, this is a Pagan symbol with layers of meanings. On the surface it is the three moon phases of waxing, full, and waning, but it also represents birth, life, and death and rebirth in the endless cycle of life. It also represents the three phases of a goddess as a maiden, mother, and crone. This symbol was

worn by high priestesses. It reminds one of the power
of the moon cycles and the wisdom that comes with
experience.

WHEEL OF LIFE: This symbol in Buddhism, also
known as the dharma wheel, represents the effects
of our states of mind in reaching nirvana. The six
divisions in the wheel represent six states of mind or
life experiences that can test us so we can liberate our
soul. It reminds one of the cycle of death and rebirth
and the journey of the soul. This is likely the most
common topic in Buddhist art, and it can be a simple
symbol or an intricate piece of art with many symbols
within it.

Using Oracle Cards to Connect to Your Spirit Guides

Each of us will find different ways to connect to spirit guides,
and some people love using oracle cards to do this. There are
many different decks that you can browse through to find one
that calls to you. You may resonate with an author who has a
blunt sense of humor or someone who simply connects to colors
and elements. I even know readers who use multiple decks
at a time to get their messages. One of the decks I connected to
early on as a reader was a deck called *The Secret Language of
Color Cards* by Inna Segal.

If you're someone who doesn't get into things unless you find
it fun and exciting, using oracle decks will likely help you connect to your spirit guides. If you're more of a systematic and
methodical person, this might frustrate you more than help

you, but you never know until you try. Just don't force it if you feel like you don't want to do it. For me, I find that different approaches call to me more at different times in my life. I used to just go out in nature and journal to connect to a message, but now I am more of a homebody and sit in bed with my journal. The point is, there's no right or wrong way to do it. You will find the connection happens easier if you are having fun.

Once you choose a deck, shuffle the cards with the intention of getting a message from your spirit guide. Keep an open mind and stop shuffling when you feel that part is complete. Spread out the cards and run your hand over the cards until you feel drawn to one. Read the message of the card in the book for the deck and look at the picture. Record anything that comes to mind in your journal, and both your impressions and the card's message will distill the message from your guides. If it doesn't make sense right now, wait, smile, and know that it soon will. Trust that your intuition will forge a connection in the other realms with the power of your intention.

One nice way to use your oracle cards as a conduit for your spirit guides is to carry them with you throughout the day. You never know when you will feel inspired to connect to spirit, and oracle cards are tools to help you do just that. When you open your heart and mind for wisdom and guidance, their images and words can help you right when you really need it. One practical application of this is when you know you're going to be around people who really test your ability to stay positive, which often is family. If you're visiting family or attending a family function, having a deck with you can allow you to stay anchored in your spiritual truth instead of getting caught up in drama.

Using Crystals to Connect to Your Spirit Guides

Arguably one of the most popular ways to connect to spirit guides is with the intuitive use of crystals. By "intuitive use" I mean that you choose a crystal that calls to you. Whether you're choosing a crystal from a store, online, or from your own collection, crystals carry a frequency that acts as a switchboard operator for where you will get the most healing. That is why it's great to just see which one draws you to it and work with that one. If you have already met multiple spirit guides, using crystals intuitively can help you connect to the guide that can help you with the most pressing healing that needs to happen in your life.

Your intuition is wise and comes from your higher self. It knows what you need to heal before your conscious mind is aware of it. It also sees your energy without the defensiveness or protectiveness of the ego and lower mind. Crystals help transmute your energy and raise your vibration so that you can see from a spiritual perspective and less of an individual perspective. When the crystals start to buffer your energy field, you will find it easier to think spiritually, which is a love frequency instead of a fear frequency.

There's no wrong crystal to work with as all crystals can help you raise your frequency. If you really want to take this crystal bridge work seriously, get a really high-powered crystal such as moldavite, phenakite, or apophyllite. Hold the crystal in meditation with the intention to connect to your guide and feel the energy of the crystal shift your energy field. You can also wear or carry the crystals with you throughout the day to connect to your guides while you're engaging with the world, which may be more challenging at first but ultimately helps you see the world and respond from a loving place.

Another way to intuitively use crystals to connect to your guides is to think of an area you'd like to work on in your life, whether it's love, healing, psychic development, communication, career, abundance, lowering anxiety, or something else. Look up a crystal that is known to help with what you'd like to work on and procure one. In meditation ask your guide to show you how to connect to the ideas that will help this issue. Your crystal will help create a bridge to allow you to perceive the ideas your guide wants to convey to you.

You can consult the appendix of meditation tools for specific crystals that have been known to help connect with certain types of guides and aid in this process.

Using Sound to Connect to Your Spirit Guides

Each of your chakras corresponds to a sound. In college I studied theater, and we used to do vocal tonings very close to each other's bodies so we could feel the sound vibrations resonate in the cavities of our own bodies. In my clairvoyant studies program, we often would do vocal toning to tune into the upper chakras and get them activated as well. Our bodies respond to harmonics and sound waves, and using specific pitches can make it much easier to connect to your spirit guides.

One way you can use sound to connect to your guides is with chakra bowls. You can play a chakra healing bowl or Tibetan singing bowl to help clear your energy and activate your chakras. You can also simply listen to chakra bowl meditation music. Certain higher-pitched tones will directly activate your upper chakras, and simply doing vocal techniques can also help stimulate the upper chakras. If you have ever been in a voice class, you will be familiar with these types of techniques. You can make sounds and try to see where you feel the sounds resonate in your body. The higher the pitch, the higher in your body it will resonate. Actors are trained to use the pitch of their voice to move emotions in humans, and sound can actually do that in your body with your own voice.

You can start by visualizing the root chakra and making a low-vibration sound and continuing up to the crown chakra, raising the pitch of the note using vowel sounds like *ooh, aah, eee.* You'll feel the resonating in your heart, throat, nasal cavity, and top of the head. It's fun, and if you're someone who likes to sing, you'll really enjoy this. This is a great thing to do when you feel like you're having trouble tuning into your meditation because it brings you into your body and gets you to start noticing subtle frequencies.

You can read more about instruments in the appendix of meditation tools.

Common Pitfalls to Avoid When Working with Spirit Guides

There are ways we try to manipulate the spirit world to fulfill our ego, and this doesn't really improve our life in any way. Knowing that this is a common side-tracking pattern that can come up can help us nip it in the bud before we miss the illusion that we are being guided by a helpful spirit guide. The ego wants instant gratification. The ego likes comforts of the flesh like sex, drugs, and rock 'n' roll. Now, I'm not saying you can't have those things, but it's not usually your spirit guide who is going to encourage you to become rich and famous. When you think you're getting a message that is going to help you get rich quickly, become a guru, save the world, or find love overnight, these are usually just the ego in disguise.

When this happens, don't panic. You have already learned a simple technique to put the ego aside in your meditations, and it really does help (when you do it). Do not get down on yourself when your ego shows up and causes confusion in your meditation. Confusion is one of the biggest signs that the ego is trying to create a diversion because it doesn't like change. On the other side of that wall of confusion is some growth that is making the ego pop up.

If your guide starts to tell you that you're somehow better than others and that you're "the chosen one," you can be pretty sure this is also the ego. While it does seem pretty obvious reading this that anything that is about our more primal desires might not be a true message from spirit, it's not always easy to pick up on. Often we set expectations that our guide is going to give us a quick fix and make us feel better right away by changing things or giving us instructions that we are used to. We are already looking for an answer that is preset in our minds, and we receive one that fulfills that expectation. While our guide is likely not going to tell us to go on a date to be happy, that is an answer the ego could disguise itself as.

The true message from spirit is energetic in nature and has to do with your own energy, attitude, and internal life and not the outside world. It doesn't have to do with raising your status or making you stand out to validate your existence. The ego might disguise itself as a plan that is all about helping people but is very focused on making lots of money. The ego can play spiritual, but you can bet if it makes you feel a rush of adrenaline, panicky, or pressured, it's not the real message from spirit that will offer you lasting strength and a sense of ease.

When you think you know what you want your guides to say, you're blocking the unknown answer they have. If you ask them yes or no questions, it can block the real and helpful perspective they have for you. For example, let's say I was trying to choose which person to date, so I ask my guides. Instead of giving me a clear answer, though, they show me a picture of dating both of them, which could be frustrating. However, instead of needing them to answer me on my terms, I can be open to a new perspective, which in this case perhaps might be just get to know them as friends and see where it goes.

We often think with tunnel vision, and one of the very amazing gifts your relationship with your spirit guides offers you is that they don't give you the answer you think you need, but they give you a whole new way of looking at things that pulls you out of your story of hardship and shows you the amazing world that awaits you. Try not to have expectations and you'll get much more out of the relationship with your guides.

Troubleshooting Your Connection with Your Spirit Guides

*D*epending on how new you are to meditation and the concept of spirit guides, you may be having some real roadblocks when it comes to connecting to your guides. Look at it this way: if you wanted to train to run in the Olympics and you just started training, it would take years to be ready, right? This practice of meditation can be developed into a real skill just like an athlete trains to compete and becomes better at it over time. If you've been meditating for years, this won't seem quite as hard, but you may be coming up against some less obvious blocks, which we will address now. After reading this chapter, you'll be better equipped to know how to handle blocks to your spiritual development and why you still may not be experiencing the spirit world.

The tips and techniques in this chapter are gathered from personal experience, in-depth trainings and studies, and being around people going through this process for over a decade. I have seen people who feel stuck and have been stuck in different ways. One thing I can say is that doubting the spirit world can come at any time, and being blocked can come at any time, but you can use that block to grow and the doubt will help you decondition another layer to reveal greater wisdom about the true nature of the universe. In many ways, it's just one big process of finding the block, recognizing and seeing what your intuition feels will help you resolve it.

In kundalini yoga, for example, often one of the major existential crisis moments hits after seven to eight years. That is when a meditation practitioner is about to break through to neutral consciousness but the shift is so big, the ego creates a big problem that seems to make it all seem fake because it senses the change coming. Having blocks is just a part of the process, but if you welcome them, know they are coming, and know they are the biggest keys to your growth and happiness, you will continue to grow as the days, weeks, months, and years pass. Then when you look back over a year or a decade you will be amazed how much your life has transformed from scared to empowered.

Browse the topics in this chapter and see if there is some area that you have completely ignored. This chapter will help you address mental, physical, and emotional areas that can be targeted to help shift your energy and continue to open your chakras. I've included some fun ways to incorporate these spiritual block-busters in your life.

Additional Chakra Healing Meditations

From an energetic approach, one of the best places to look when you're not connecting with your guides is at the chakras. These two meditations help with two common issues that can block the energy flow you need in order to access your spirit guides in the upper chakras. If you think of your chakras like an energy circuit, it makes sense that if one is blocking the flow, the light bulb cannot turn on. The first meditation is a guided visualization to help you use your intention to unblock your chakras.

The second meditation addresses what many of us also experience as adults, which can be called "being jaded." When we feel unmotivated to go out and find love and romance or that all relationships are hard and doomed to fail, that indicates a block in the heart chakra that will not allow energy to travel to the upper chakras, which need to be active in order to access a relationship with your spirit guides.

Any feelings of grief, sadness, jealousy, self-pity, codependence, or just lack of feeling altogether could indicate that from one or more of your experiences, this chakra has shut down temporarily. Don't worry! Once we get it back online, things will start to shift and you'll experience that opening of your heart, which helps you feel new growth in your life and a return of optimism to engage and find love again.

Just as an athlete would need to fix a broken bone in order to run in a race, you also need to fix a blocked chakra in order to access higher states of consciousness. It's not that hard, and you can start by doing some meditations and continue by using the other approaches I offer as well. This meditation is like a maintenance meditation. To fix what is leaking or malfunctioning, we must first decide to do it. Even if you're new to this concept, try to approach it with an open mind. Energy is not visible like plumbing in a house but it does keep you feeling good when it's working well. Sometimes when a chakra unblocks, you'll get a rush of heat in that area.

Sit in a comfortable position or lie down for this meditation. Begin to slow and deepen your breath, allowing yourself to relax and come into your body more and more. Start to go within yourself, the vast inner world of consciousness where all your feelings and thoughts can be navigated and seen.

Bring your awareness to your root chakra at the base of the spine. See if it feels alive with vibrant life-force energy or if it feels somehow off. Your intuition will sense something so just trust it. If it feels off, ask the universe to fill it with light and remove any block to this chakra right now. Visualize white light coming into this chakra and restoring it to a vibrant red, giving you the energy you need to feel grounded. See how you feel after allowing this shift.

Take a deep breath in and move your awareness up to the sacral chakra, just below the navel. See if the energy here feels vibrant and healthy or if something feels tense or off. Ask the universe to remove any block to this chakra and fill it with healing light right now. Visualize the chakra as a vibrant and balanced orange color, giving you the energy you need to feel joy.

Move your awareness to the upper stomach now as you breathe deeply in and out of your nose. Tune into your solar plexus chakra here and notice what the energy is like. Does it feel vibrant or low? Ask the universe to send healing light to this chakra now and lift any block from this chakra. Breathe as you see this chakra a golden yellow filled with universal life-force energy, allowing you to feel optimism and confidence.

On your next breath, bring your awareness to the heart, lungs, and chest area. Notice what the energy feels like when you tune into the space of your heart chakra. Feel into the energy to see if it feels light and energized or heavy and dull. Ask the universe to send healing light to this area right now and remove any blocks impeding the flow of energy for your self-love and connection to others. Visualize the chakra now glowing a beautiful green.

Check in with your breathing and deepen it now as you bring your focus to the throat area. What do you feel is the quality of the energy of your throat chakra at this moment? Ask the universe to infuse it with healing white light and dislodge any energetic blocks in this area right now. Visualize a pure blue light now filling this space. As it clears, sense the openness of your communication and the freedom with which you can share your ideas. Also sense the connection opening to spiritual communication as you take a deep breath and feel the cool air in your throat.

You're doing great, and you are working with the energy of the cosmos to heal. Your goal to connect to your spirit guides is being realized.

With your next deep breath, shift your focus up to the mystical third eye at the brow point. How does the energy feel as you focus here? Does it feel open or closed? Flowing or tangled? Ask the universe to bless you with healing light directly to your third eye chakra right now and remove any impediments to having this chakra open. Notice a brilliant purple or indigo light now filling the area of your third eye.

You've stepped across the threshold to the spirit world, and you have one more key to unlock. With your next deep breath, bring your awareness to the crown chakra at the top of the skull. How does this area feel when you tune into it? Call on the universe to send its healing vibration directly to this space to open you to the spirit world and heal the flow of divine energy. See a beautiful white or violet light hovering above your head, connecting you to the unseen realm with ease.

Feel the flow of energy moving freely between all of the energy centers, the earth, and spirit. You are coming into alignment and allowing your soul to enter your life.

~

Well done. Take a deep breath to return to where you're sitting, and write down anything that stood out about this experience.

The heart chakra is the largest energy center and also one that must be healed in order to break the illusion of duality created by the ego. Once this chakra is flowing, your energy can access the upper chakras, where you can actually feel bliss, connection to all of life, and overcome the fear of death.

The heart chakra sits between the upper and lower chakras, and this midpoint is often tied to some of the most challenging relationships and experiences we've had. Without having to relive those hardships, you will be able to start using the power of your intention to remove low-vibration energy from this area's cellular memory. Using the breath and visualization, progress can be made to free you from dense vibrations here so you can continue on the path of the great journey to meet your spirit guides and heal with them.

Start by taking three deep breaths. As you exhale, release your sadness and honor it. You're already starting to release the buildup in this space. Sit tall as you continue to breathe deeply in and out of your nose. Envision a vibrant green coming into your body with each deep breath. It goes to the heart chakra and starts to loosen the grip of the lower vibrations in this space. The green is love, compassion, and deep connection to the core of creation.

With each breath, the grip of the lower vibrations loosens and you start to sense them being released out of your energy field. Continue to visualize the green energy releasing this stuck energy as you breathe deeply and slowly. This gentle unfolding, this calm renaissance of your soul, is divine awakening to your true essence. The love of being free from self-hatred is growing with each breath. You are pure love—pure consciousness wanting to give love.

Ask the universe to help you strengthen and heal your heart so you can grow, open to love, and have safe boundaries. Thank the universe for hearing your request and giving you its support. Now just sit in this new energy, feeling the strength and power of the heart center, this huge magnetic forcefield of love that will guide you like a compass to the right decisions.

~

Well done. You're healing and growing, and you've made great progress today.

Take a deep breath and come back to the place you're sitting. Write down anything that you felt in your heart area as you did this and anything that may have surprised you as you healed this chakra today.

Healing with Reiki

Sometimes you can do all the meditations, wear all the crystals, and still not connect to your guides. If your nervous system doesn't have enough energy, your energy will feel dim and low. It will not be enough to meditate and keep trying to access your third eye. You'll need to add some prana, whether that is through breathwork or with the help of a Reiki practitioner (or both). Prana, the life-force energy also known as qi or chi, will allow you to rejuvenate your nervous system after trauma or prolonged stress. Sometimes getting the motivation to do a daily breathwork practice just feels like too much because energy is already so low. If that is the case, booking an in-person or distance Reiki session can be the next best step. Consider it an energetic maintenance tune-up that will help cleanse the gunk from your energy field.

Reiki is a powerful healing modality that works directly with your chakras to unblock them and charge them. Someone else allows energy to flow through their energy field and directs it to each of your chakras until they start to flow again. It is a painless process that starts to heal your nervous system right away. There are three levels of Reiki practitioners, and once someone is a Reiki Master, they are able to share more energy. It's good to look around and see how different people make you feel when you consider getting a session with them. Someone who is a dedicated practitioner and very experienced will likely be able to offer a better session than someone who is just getting their feet wet in Eastern medicine.

In a session it's common to have memories flash before your eyes that you haven't thought of in a while. Often tears will just start to flow and sometimes muscles twitch or you'll feel heat and a slight pressure where the practitioner is working. They may get an image of the memory blocking a chakra and be able to use their training to heal the chakra. It's not always an instant fix, although you'll likely feel lighter and more energetic after the session, as if you're more clear-minded. The week or two following can include tiredness, emotional swings, and flu-like detox symptoms as the body adjusts to the new frequency and stabilizes. Having multiple sessions is a good idea to continue to heal your energy.

If you are having trouble connecting to your guides, it may be due to a number of reasons. Your energy may be low because of diet, thought patterns, toxins, and low energy. The Reiki session is merely the loving, healing energy of the universe that will help you align your energy to start seeing how to shift your decisions to harmonize your overall energy. It's subtle, but over the course of a few months, it really makes a difference and can help when you feel blocked or even depressed.

Activating the Third Eye

If you are not seeing images in your third eye yet, that is nothing to be concerned about. Don't give up. Understanding what blocks the third eye and how to unblock it will get you where you want to be, which is perceiving and working with your spirit guides. The third eye is the pineal gland. When it is blocked, it is because there are usually nanocrystals around it that are blocking the communication and perception function. These nanocrystals can be dislodged by removing fluoride from your toothpaste and water and by using specific foods and plants that will help to remove them.

Additionally, vibrating the pineal gland will help it to activate. We will discuss how to use certain chanting techniques and sound therapies to start vibrating this gland and get it to start working for you.

Diet and Herbs

One approach that can help you open your third eye is to clean up your diet. By making choices that are healthier and shifting to less processed foods, your body will begin a natural detox process. Drinking lots of water and thinking about how each thing you consume nourishes you can help your physical body support your meditation practice. While it's common in the spiritual community to do intense cleanses without food, that can be an emotional roller coaster and add to your stress unnecessarily. Cleanses like that can be hard to sustain while working as your energy often drops, leading to emotional outbursts or lethargy followed by elation. This can be hard for coworkers to deal with as well as yourself because it shocks your body.

A more gradual approach can be looking to incorporate more plants into your diet over time, and as your taste buds change, they will start to taste better. Eating more fruits and vegetables, nuts, seeds, legumes, and superfoods can really jump-start the opening of your third eye. In fact, this is probably what I attribute my own third eye opening to the most. Raw foods are full of prana and extremely nutrient dense so they help you in an energetic and physical sense. When you start to increase the nutrient level in your food, your body has what it needs to function optimally and feeling good becomes easier, hence accessing higher states of consciousness does as well. However, when you're making that transition, knowing what to eat can be a bit of a challenge.

Using herbs and spices to make food taste good will help you enjoy the process of falling in love with natural foods. Finding recipes that you want to try will help you not fall into the trap of feeling like all you can eat is bland lettuce. Also, don't do it all at once because your body needs time to adjust. You still need healthy fats like coconut, nuts, butter or vegan butter, avocado, and oils to have energy. If you don't get enough calories or you don't have fat, you will quickly become tired, irritable, and want to give up. The problem with juice cleanses is that they create such a roller coaster of emotions and energy that it feels like punishment, and we want to avoid things that don't feel good. My best advice is to make healthy food delicious and find the joy of it.

Certain foods and herbs, such as oregano oil, are also known to help decalcify the pineal gland. Oregano oil is very potent and must be taken as recommended, and you must be careful not to get it in your eyes or on sensitive skin membranes (it's like hot peppers in that way). Lemons are another great option for decalcifying the pineal gland. Drinking fresh squeezed lemon juice for about ten days can make a big difference. Foods with deep pigments that are dark green or purple are considered the most nutrient rich and can be some of the most efficient foods to help open your third eye. Making smoothies with superfoods and spinach can be a delicious path to enlightenment, and salads with a variety of plants and healthy dressing can also substitute other processed foods that contain chemicals, preservatives, and many toxic ingredients that block your spiritual growth.

Ultimately, the more clean you eat and drink, the easier it will be to feel good, access the upper chakras, and meet your guides. Don't think of it as eliminating good stuff but finding even more rich and alive flavors through a variety of natural flavors and the art of cooking. Certain herbs can also help you activate your pineal gland and have been used for a very long time to access the spiritual realms. You do not need to take hallucinogens (entheogens) to access the spirit world, although some do.

A safe way to use herbs is by drinking tea that is readily available online but not usually in stores. These intuition-opening herbs are potent and completely legal, unlike most entheogens. Their effect is also not as strong, so you are not putting yourself at risk. Some herbs will interact with medications or are not recommended while pregnant or breastfeeding, so please consider this before consuming them. Teas using mugwort, rose, lavender, and star anise are known to help stimulate the upper chakras. Detox tea and digestion-aiding tea like ginger can also help harmonize the mind-body connection. Lowering your intake of sugar, caffeine, and alcohol and replacing all or most of it with herbal tea can be one step in the right direction. Alkaline water from a store that removes fluoride or a brand that offers artesian well water can also be a new habitual drink that will help lower inflammation and aid in decalcifying the pineal gland.

Meditation

A simple meditation you can do for a few weeks that will help your third eye is chanting. The sound of ONG, which is more directly stimulated to the pineal gland than OM, will help stir this gland to life. If you chant it for ten minutes a day, you may start to get the white flashing light or subtle energetic sensations that indicate your third eye is opening. Elongate the *ong*, taking a deep breath between each one and feeling where the sound vibrates in your skull. The *om* sound vibrates the chest and mouth, but the *ong* sound vibrates higher up in the nasal cavity. Just as you shake someone to wake them or make a piano string or guitar string vibrate to produce sound, vibrating the pineal gland helps it switch on.

Additionally, you may want to think about how much time you spend in meditation each day and simply increase it. If you're meditating five minutes a day, it is going to prove very difficult to get into a deep brain wave state where your body is relaxed enough to even get used to guided meditation. The consistency of your meditation and the length of your meditation might be just the missing link for you. If you are struggling with the idea that it is boring, give yourself a fighting chance at least and go back to the meditations at the beginning of the book. Spend more time with them and try. It's not about being a perfect meditator; it's about making an effort while also just being relaxed and having a sense of fun and lightness about it.

If you just can't seem to get into a meditative state by yourself, that's okay too. Join a meditation group where the group energy will help you reach a deeper state. This is energetic assistance when you're in a group because the vibration of those who have a big energy field and go into deep states of meditation quickly will link up with everyone else's energy fields and help you get into a deep meditative state. In my own experience, I was able to reach very deep states of meditation in a group first and then at home. I value the group meditation experience for progress in energetic awakening just as highly as I value diet and herbs.

Sound Healing

Going to a sound healing at a yoga studio can start to help your nervous system enter a relaxed state. The more you incorporate healing sound into your day, the more you will begin to get used to relaxation. Sound healings in a yoga studio often involve different soothing instruments like crystal singing bowls, rainsticks, gongs, drums, and sitars that provide sound waves that hit your energy field and start to create harmony in your energy field. A disrupted energy field is caused by stress and habitual thoughts of negativity.

If you want to get a crystal singing bowl and use it at home, that also can be effective and helpful. There are many ways to access sound healing with modern technology. Meditation music is readily available for free online, and certain frequencies can help induce a meditative state. "Binaural beats" and "Hemi-Sync" are terms you can search for to find music that can help you practice deep relaxation. Mantras can also help to create an energy field prime for meditation. Recordings of kundalini yoga mantras are based on the yogic science of naad, which is the in-depth study of how sounds in certain combinations can create new brain patterns that allow us to overcome negative patterns. Listening to them or chanting them can have an equally strong effect. Try using the same mantra each day for a month and notice how your energy starts to shift.

Ultimately sound is moving energy in our subconscious to help clear it and create new positive associations with life. There is no exact time that will indicate your third eye will officially be open from sound healing because it is a subtle process that is like a mental detox from thought patterns. Playing mantras and meditation music in your home, car, and at work can actually work on your energy all day and night, and this is a technique used by many advanced meditators and spiritual healers. It is hard for the mind to grasp how sound shifts your consciousness so I advise to try it for a month and see how different you feel.

Affirmations to Open to Spirit Guides

Very similar to how sound waves interact with and assist our energetic detox is the power of intention. All guided meditations are harnessing the power of intention, and using very carefully chosen words in repetition is one of the oldest and most common forms of consciousness training used by spiritual systems worldwide. Mantras, prayers, incantations, and even spells use the power of words to harness our intention and create new patterns that our consciousness can live within.

Using these affirmations daily for a few weeks can be a very simple, straightforward way to override any subconscious thoughts that are blocking you from opening to the spirit world or adapting a lifestyle that will allow you to do so. You may try writing the affirmation you choose to work with twenty times each morning and night or perhaps you want to practice reciting it as often as possible throughout the day. Placing an affirmation around your home can help it become a habitual thought pattern because some of us are visual learners. If you're an auditory learner, you may like the idea of recording the affirmation for five minutes and then listening to it each day.

Here are some affirmations that target different types of energy and outcomes all related to working with your spirit guides. Read through them and see which one or ones seem to pull your attention the most and you'll know which one to start working with.

I have a strong connection to my spirit guides.

My spirit guides are my closest friends.

My spirit guides help me see the energy of each decision to make the best choice.

I am a soul living in communion with the spirit world to help others.

I have a spiritual lifestyle where my connection to spirit is my top priority.

My favorite thing to do is meditate.

Every challenge is an opportunity to grow with the help of the spiritual realm.

I'm making better choices with the help of my loving spirit guides.

I'm excited to meet my spirit guides each day.

There is great power in awakening to one's soul and spirit guides.

*My soul communicates in feelings and my spirit guides
communicate through my soul.*

*I'm growing spiritually every day and opening my
third eye work with high-vibrational beings.*

Vision Board Activity to Open to Spirit Guides

Vision boarding is a technique used widely in the spiritual community because it harnesses the power of your intention by stimulating your senses and giving you a tangible act to create something that is tied to a vision and emotional response. A vision board is simply a board of cardboard, cork, wood, poster board, etc., that holds images and words that clearly indicate your goal. Vision boards are manifesting tools that activate the law of attraction through your senses, and creating a visual representation helps you clarify your goal while also giving you a reminder of your goal to see daily.

Vision boards are often thought of for manifesting things we want in the physical world such as a house, car, boyfriend, etc., but they are just as helpful when it comes to manifesting spiritual and emotional things. If you find your focus is all over the place in your life, that is totally normal! We all have our finances, health, relationships, career, friendships, hobbies, and other things pulling on our focus. That is exactly why making a vision board is essential and transformational in your spiritual progress and will aid in opening your connection to your spirit guides. When we want to be a rock star, we put up a poster of our favorite rock star on the wall to remind us to practice our guitar, right? It's the same with developing the connection to your spirit guides: you have to remind yourself and inspire yourself frequently by making it a point to set your mind in the desired direction of having this bond.

Here are simple steps to create a vision board, which you can do on your own or with friends.

STEP 1: Gather scissors, markers, magazines, tape, glue, stickers, glitter, and anything else that you feel inspired by. Get a piece of cardboard or poster board and sit down for a meditation before you begin. This creation process should be very intentional and not rushed.

STEP 2: Breathe slowly and deeply as you ask the universe to help you create a board that will inspire you to connect with your guides. Whatever actions will help you do that in your daily life might show up as you ask the universe for guidance and inspiration for how to approach making this board. You may get inspired and you may not. Don't overthink it.

STEP 3: As you look through the magazines, stay focused on wanting to connect to your guides and see what images or words stand out to you. Cut them out and place them on your board without adhering them yet. Don't rush but think about anything else you may feel inspired to include on your board. You may want to write a word, include a picture of a spiritual figure, or simply add something that you feel will help you heal and feel good about life. Sometimes the path to opening up is self-love and sometimes it's drinking more water. Simple things or abstract goals are all fair game.

STEP 4: Glue or tape the images and words on your board in any way that you feel inspired. This is creating an energy that gives you an emotional response you will get each time you look at the board. Perhaps a reminder to take time for yourself, to create boundaries, or take bubble baths will help you shift; it's going to be unique to where you are in your life now and what feels healing. You can also simply put your goal to connect to your spirit guides on it. Some people have a busy board and some keep it simple.

STEP 5: Place your vision board by your bed where you will see it each morning and night. Your vision board should be afforded a place of honor and not hidden away. This represents the most important progress and goal in your life, and if you make it important by framing it and putting it on a spiritual altar, it will hold that much more emotional gravity to attract what you want.

Use your vision board by sitting in front of it each morning and night and holding the intention. Visualize what it's like to be in that space where it's natural and easy to connect to your guides. Feel the feelings of trust and ease that will come when it has manifested to open yourself to this reality and project the idea into your subconscious. This will help shift your habits and use of time to allow you to prioritize this and open to the parts of your mind that tune into the spiritual realm.

Healing with Your Spirit Guides

*H*aving a rich inner world allows you to be stronger than the external world and maneuver in it energetically, accepting what you experience, releasing it, and elevating your consciousness. This unlocks the secrets of time beyond the linear path of consciousness so you can see your past, present, and future in a more fluid way. This also allows you to experience the eternal present, which is full of joy. Many times your guides will give you ways to become more present by finding things you enjoy immersing yourself in such as being in nature, cooking, exercising, and listening to music.

In your work with your guides, similar to how we work with tarot, having an intention can help you. Bringing a question to your guides that will help you heal can allow you to see in a new way. With tarot we get a lot more when we ask specific types of open-ended questions and not yes or no questions. For example, we can ask how to best direct our energy to open to love instead of if we will find love by the end of the month. Because your guides are already aware that everything is energy, they can help you get past your mind to see how to heal on an energetic level. The questions posed in these meditations will help you foster a valuable relationship with your guides that you have met and those you have yet to meet.

Much of the work you will do with your spirit guides in regard to healing is a process of deconditioning. Deconditioning is removing the layers of illusion that you have been programmed to accept as reality. Some examples of this that are easy to see in our world include cult brainwashing scenarios where people realize they are being manipulated and escape by changing what they previously accepted as true. We've seen many celebrities who were involved in Scientology come forward and talk about this. Some people, like those involved with David Koresh in Waco, were not so lucky, and many practicing Seventh Day Adventists still do not know he was in an offshoot of that religion or know the full history. The point here is that we become naturalized and normalized into our environment without being aware of it.

Throughout history, this is how cultures have formed webs of significance and ascribed meaning to things in order to establish barter systems with currency and create societies where people accept the value of services. However helpful this process of societal consensus can be in making life easier so that we do not all have to hunt, prepare, and grow our own food, it can also be harmful when we are not aware that we are buying into a system of thought. Radicalization, homophobia, sexism, xenophobia, addiction, racism, and misogyny are examples of these conditionings that we can recognize as harmful to society. The deep levels of conditioning that come from a philosophical basis about gender roles, for example, give us the "happily ever after" idea that many people never even question.

While we may be able to recognize toxic conditioning based on these types of labels, it's harder to spot in our own minds. Much of what you will do with your spirit guides is stop seeing the world as something that is happening to you. In a very positive light, spirit guides show you how everything is energy and that the physical world is the slowest and densest form of energy. This means you'll be able to see beyond the veil that makes most people live in fear, buy into cultural normalizations, and feel pressured to fit in so they don't become ostracized and lose their "power." Much of this has to do with being able to see how we behave in ways that perpetuate harmful cultural practices that hurt our own well-being. For example, participating in a habit of eating unhealthy foods can steal your energy and emotional well-being, and you never may have questioned this normalized behavior until your spirit guide started to show you that you can. They are here to give you power over your thoughts, behaviors, and choices.

For the meditations in this chapter, the guide may vary depending on which guide shows up for you. Sometimes multiple guides will show up to work with you on a meditation and that's fine as well. These meditations use plural guides for ease, but know that there is some wiggle room because spirit shows up creatively.

Healing from Some of the Toughest Things in Life with Spirit Guides

Many of you have been through tragedies and things that are difficult to think and talk about. Your habits in life may be hurting you, and you may not be aware of it because it is all you have seen. No matter how hard things have been up to this point in your life, you found this book for a reason and your guides will help you find inner strength to change your energy and your thoughts and truly heal. You may currently feel powerless in your home, your job, or your love life, but your spirit guides, with the help of your higher self, will show you that you are powerful beyond what you can conceive.

If you have experienced a violent or unstable household, bullying, insecurities, or heartbreak, reading this book is right where you need to be. Those traumas can cause emotional pressure that can cause depression, anxiety, and a cycle of repeating patterns that cause you to seek happiness outside of yourself because it's all you know as far as where to go for happiness. Your guides will show you and give you the experience of finding happiness from inside yourself, the vast life of your inner world. They will guide you to shift your thoughts and emotions over time so you no longer need a person, object, or title to feel content. They will invert your search for happiness, giving you back your power and breaking toxic patterns in the process. This is a process of love, discovery, and expansion that will only enhance your life.

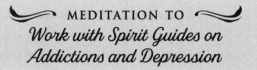

Many of us get used to a baseline of addictions and depression in our life because everyone we know is mildly depressed and self-medicating with food, drugs, sex, and alcohol. Depression and addiction don't just happen to older people. It often starts in youth and becomes something we think that we have to live with. We feel crushed by the weight of the world and carry this weight, not knowing we do not have to.

This meditation may help you lift an energy pattern you're unaware you're participating in. It may help you physically, and it may also help you align to a more fulfilling life that has a spiritual perspective. Sometimes our addiction is to ideas implanted by the ego that make us chase things that really offer us only a void of emotional gratification. These addictions can be subtle and stealthy even when we have been on our spiritual path for a while and think we are addiction-free.

To begin this meditation, sit with a straight spine so the energy can run easily between each chakra. Start to breathe slowly and deeply, allowing your mind and body to relax. Get in touch with your energy field by visualizing your aura and seeing how your energy feels at this moment. Is it heavy? Is it light and bright? Does it feel off-kilter? Just notice without judgment as you breathe and relax.

Now go within yourself and let the outside world fade away. Meet your guides in your usual space and ask them what thoughts or perspectives you are having that are creating negative psychic pressure in your life. Often a perspective is the root of a behavior. Wait for an image, idea, or word to come to you and write it down. Ask your guides how this is affecting you on an energetic level and then allow them to heal that energy by asking them to help you lift it away from your consciousness. This freeing process allows you to raise your vibration to see a new possible reality.

Now that you're free of this thought pattern, you can see how light you feel and how you can now see a new direction that is more optimal for your energy and emotional well-being. You do not have to blame any external circumstance; you get to see how simply shifting your thoughts changes the direction of the wind blowing your sails and guiding your ship. Thank your spirit guides and ask them if there is something you can focus on to help you heal this aspect of your life. It may be something simple: a healthy food, a mantra, a habit, or a state of mind. Write it down and thank them for helping you heal on this deep energetic level today.

Take three deep breaths to bring yourself back to the room. Write down anything else you would like to and reflect on how your spirit guides are able to direct you to a more loving reality.

Great job on doing this. It would be nice for you to do something to take a break emotionally now such as have a snack, take a walk, or do some simple stretching.

This meditation will allow your spirit guides to show you a way to cultivate self-love and healthy boundaries. Often we allow someone else's stress or burdens to affect our energy, and we are pulled down from one person's drama to the next. Sometimes we are striving to be positive and yet feel pulled out of our positivity by one person who just gets in and makes us feel negative. That person may be someone you see on a regular basis or it may be memories that haunt you and steal your happiness. This is something that you can shift with the help of the spirit world.

Your spirit guides will help you shift your energy and heal the energy that allows someone else to overpower your happiness. Just how they do that is yet to be seen, but it will be something that feels right for you. So let's dive in and get you back to feeling great. Feel free to use this meditation as often as you need to.

Start by taking a deep breath in your nose and out of your mouth, relaxing as you breathe out slowly. Go ahead and do that two more times, letting go of the racing thoughts and tension in your body. You are now going to enter the loving co-creation space with your guides that will allow you to retrieve your energy and rejuvenate your vitality. They are ready and waiting to help you, and this particular subject will be one you find frees you to feel much more excited about life again. Now that you're in the company of your spirit guides, ask them to show you which relationship is most important to work on today so you can feel the most uplifted.

Allow them to tune you into the energy of this relationship and just notice how it feels. You'll probably sense why this one is the most important to work with. Breathe slowly and deeply and ask your guide to help you shift the energy between you and this person from one of judgment to one of compassion. Each part of the memory will now be transmuted from judgment to compassion. Judgment to compassion—you see it changing the color of the energy that has been affecting you. The colors start to have a more healed appearance and feeling.

Now it's time to ask your guides what role this person should have in your life moving forward. How much, if at all, should they be in your life in order for you to feel safe, loved, and respected? Wait and see what message your guides provide you with and write it down. If you need clarification, ask for it. Allow yourself to notice if this message feels like the best choice for you. Now, in your mind's eye, ask the universe to help you create a bubble of loving, positive energy around you so that that person's energy bounces off of you and is returned to them in a loving way. Your deflection will protect

your thoughts and allow you to focus on your
soul's purpose without interlocking with them.

Your spirit guides will show you something that helps
you see this person on a soul level so you can forgive
them. You don't have to hate them or change them.
Your job is to make sure you're making decisions
that are self-loving. Your own energy is most helpful
to the world when it is peaceful and not trying to
force people to change. Your own energy is also most
helpful to the world when you establish healthy
boundaries that allow you the space to be yourself.

Ask your spirit guides to continue helping you lift
your vibration throughout the day today as you get
used to this bubble that deflects negative energy. Ask
them to help you not blame anyone for how you're
feeling. Remember to ask your guides for help staying
in a state of self-love. Thank your guides and take
three deep breaths to return to the place you're sitting.

Stay still for a while as you reflect on the meditation and write
down how things feel like they have shifted.

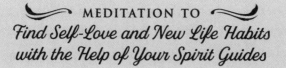

Find Self-Love and New Life Habits with the Help of Your Spirit Guides

Spirit guides can help you recover and heal your self-esteem. They also help you simplify your life and desires so you can be happy now. We often put our happiness at some point in the future when we attain a certain goal, but your spirit guides can help you see that a story where you never get to be happy unless something happens really isn't self-loving. They help you see any ideas, goals, or motivations that are weighing you down by making it seem like happiness is a complicated thing far in the future.

In this meditation you will begin to be able to see how you complicate your happiness and how to simplify what you need in order to be happy. You'll be able to let go of the ideas of yourself that involve comparison in the present, guilt over the past, or nonacceptance of yourself in any way. This is a big, exciting step in your great journey with your spirit guides, and it is something you can do over and over again to continue to decondition from the insecurities blocking you from happiness in this very moment.

Begin by taking three deep breaths to release all tension in your body. On each exhale, think *relax*. Now continue breathing slowly and deeply as you go within yourself and let the external world fade from your mind. Your deep well of healing is ready and waiting for you. You will meet your guide in your usual place and ask them what ideas are blocking you from feeling happy right now. Wait and just observe without rushing this process. If something shows up and it isn't clear to you, ask for clarification.

If you feel afraid to see it, it's probably something deeply ingrained that will change your life in a major way. Once you see the idea that is blocking your happiness, practice not having that idea and see how much lighter you feel. This shows you the freedom available to you with a simple decision. This is a safe way to hypothetically see a new outlook on life. This is not laziness or shirking responsibility; it's reorganizing your priorities to align with spiritual growth instead of egoistic desires that do not provide you the happiness you deserve.

Write down the idea that your spirit guides showed you, even if it doesn't yet make sense. They will show you something that helps unlock the answer, even if it takes a little more time. They know how to help you heal, so trust the process. If they don't give you a clear answer, it may mean that you are blocking yourself from the healing process because your ego is afraid of the change in your core beliefs. Try putting your ego in its mansion and return to your spirit guides, asking them to help you see how to live happily in the present moment all the time. You have the ability to share love and light, and they will help you return to that as the true source of eternal happiness.

Thank your spirit guides for their guidance and
wisdom accepting the process, however it unfolded.

~

Take a deep breath and come back to where you're sitting, and
write down anything you would like to remember or that stood
out to you. Then take a break and maybe shake out your body
with some sounds to loosen up.

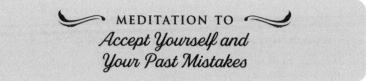

A lot of the negative energy we hold in our energy field is stored memories and opinions about ourselves that separate us from our spiritual identity and happiness. When our thoughts are constantly trying to keep up with the proverbial Kardashians, we aren't in the flow of our spirit and our vibration continues to lower, allowing us to fall into the habits of fear-based living where we think we have to prove our worthiness in order to be happy and gain approval from the outside world. No matter how much you think you have messed up, you can uncover your self-love, your spiritual identity, and heal your happiness.

Your spirit guides are excited to help you accept yourself and heal from the past with this meditation. Prepare for the meditation by finding a place where it feels like the energy is uplifting. Perhaps prepare the space a little to make it feel ready for meditation. Taking time to prepare your space can help you really experience a deep, transformational meditation. Tuning into the energy of your space is also a great practice to help you start to notice energy and what environments help you stay uplifted.

Begin to slow and deepen your breath, breathing through your nose. Feel the tension in your body begin to melt with each breath as the prana and life-giving force of the universe raise your vibration to prepare you to meet your spirit guide. Allow the outside world to fade as you tune into the vast internal world that is the source of your spiritual strength, healing, and growth in this life.

You will now meet your spirit guides and allow them to take you on a journey to one revealing moment in time that is stealing your happiness and weighing you down. It will reveal how you are accepting negative self-talk based on this memory. Wait and let it be shown to you. The sting that this memory has is no longer going to have power over you. Your spirit guides are beckoning you to release the energy that has been stored in your energy field related to this and the way it has blocked you from seeing that you are pure, radiant spiritual love worthy of joy and total self-acceptance.

Write down what you are shown and then ask your spirit guides to help you release all energy related to this right now. With a few deep breaths, feel the energy leave as you are freed from this thought.

Feel the love for your true spiritual soul rush in and heal the parts of your consciousness that have been holding that energy. You are healing. You are recovering your energy and becoming whole, aware of your spiritual truth and your true power to generate your happiness by choosing what you focus on in each moment. Thank your spirit guides

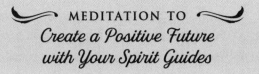

A part of the healing that your guides can help you with is creating a vision that aligns with your soul that heals the energy you're projecting into the future. When a psychic picks up on your future, it's purely based on the current energy you're holding and the likely outcome that energy is creating. In that light, you are able to shift your energy, with the help of your loving spirit guides, to create a future that feels uplifting, inspiring, and truly peaceful. This can help you break the cycles of negative experiences that can come from unconsciously expecting more bad things to come your way. This type of energetic overhaul is fun, and sometimes it takes practice to actually believe you have much more control over your destiny than what most people think.

For this meditation, you will want to really allow time between the instructions to see what your guides want to show you. Get your journal and cue your calming meditation music so that you can really enter a deep meditative state. You're doing the sacred work with your guides that will help you see new potential and new levels of happiness that await you. This is really getting you to the next level in your life, where you're able to feel the optimism that comes from having a real relationship with the spirit world and using your spiritual identity as your compass.

⌒

Sit in a comfortable position with a straight spine.
Begin to breathe slowly and deeply as you relax
your body and let go of your thoughts. Begin the
visualization by putting your ego self in its mansion
so that you can work more easily with your higher self
and spirit guides. Allow your higher self to meet you
and take you to meet the guides who will work with
you on creating a vision of your future that is healthy,
high vibrational, and in the highest good for you and
for the evolution of the planet.

Once your higher self introduces you to the guides
who will be working with you, see if the guides want to
take you to a special place where you can return to see
your future, the one you are creating and manifesting
that is based on love, spiritual awareness, and the
truth in your heart. First you may see something that
represents your old goals that no longer align with
your energy. You can, with the help of your guide,
release this older energy with gratitude, for that
energy served you during the past. Now you're going
to allow your guides to help you raise your vibration
to see the future that excites your soul and inspires
your heart. What do you see? Write it down. Just wait
and observe all the details your guides reveal to you
as they help create an energetic bridge of perception.

Hold this vision and notice how you feel when you focus on this. Does it feel different than what you've set as goals before? Does it feel like there's a real connection to the core of your being when you focus on this? Thank your guides and return to your higher self. As you walk away, feel the new excitement you have to live. Feel the desire to spread joy that is in your cells. This is a sort of rebirthing of your spirit— a momentous occasion! You are finding your way. You're on the great journey with the help of your spirit team. Thank your higher self and take a deep breath to come back to the place you're sitting.

~

Write down anything else that stood out or that you'd like to remember. Relax and allow yourself to tune into your body to see what it needs in this moment.

7

Manifesting with Your Spirit Guides

Spirit guides help you experience your power and tap into your ability to create. This chapter could be done over the course of a weekend or perhaps in a day, taking breaks between the meditations. It's always up to you how you use these meditations, but now that you're working on something more light and exciting, you may feel doing more than one meditation helps build positive momentum that helps fuel a real shift in your life.

Your guides work with you based on the law of attraction. The law of attraction is a higher law of the universe that governs the energy within all things. It is based on the premise that like attracts like, so when we are equipped with this axiom, we are able to attract the energy we generate. In more direct terms, if we are sad, we attract people who reflect that state. If we are expectant of great things, we will resonate with and meet people in that high-vibration amplified state as well. Earlier in the book we used this knowledge to help us start to heal our vibration by clearing low vibrations stored in our subconscious. Now we will use our intention to generate a state that is desired and help charge the visions we hold for our future.

While it can be easy to say something like "I want a great job, a happy family, and money to spare," getting clear on the goals that align with your soul is often more of a tricky endeavor. As we have also discussed, the ego often directs us to want things that are more about instant gratification than long-term sustained spiritual inspiration and stability, the latter being the one that is desired is one that your spirit guides can help you hone in on. Consider your spirit guides as beacons helping you track your greatest fulfillment in life. As they blink, you follow their frequency right to the gold mine of your soul.

Working with Spirit Guides Is Magical

You're now getting to the part of the great journey with your guides where you're stepping more into your power, your ability to actually use real magic. Chances are if you're reading this book, the archetypes of mystical beings have drawn your curiosity for a while, and now you get the honor of working with those energies. This path is not to be taken lightly, as the saying holds true that with great power comes great responsibility. The use of magic and knowing how to manifest must be done responsibly and ethically or the law of cause and effect, which is another higher law of the universe, will bring any intentions that are selfish, immoral, or inconsiderate right back to you.

This is not something to be afraid of; it's just a very candid statement that you must use your power and knowledge of the spirit world for good means.

We are able to attract resources we need, manifest great things, change our circumstances, and call on higher spiritual beings to give us wisdom to navigate decisions. With the help of your guides, you'll find that you have much more power than you can possibly use in your lifetime. Getting hung up on the fact that you can manifest is not the point. The whole endeavor of working with your guides is to get you to a place where you naturally want to help the greater good and feel best doing that. Trust that the relationship between your mind, intuition, and spiritual team will get you there.

Once you go through these meditations, you can expect to have a clearer picture of the future your soul wants you to step into, a plan to get there, and the energy to fuel that journey.

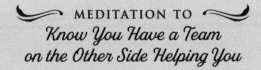

As you embark on the journey to awaken and use your magic, your inner world will become the most important part of that process. This is where you will go to fuel the vision, where you will find the vision, and where you will find the support to navigate the energetic realms. The inner world is far more important than the outer world when it comes to manifesting. You must have the inner world alive and vivid in order to really maneuver in the physical world. You'll still have plenty of time to work toward your goals in the real world and will need to but up until now, you've not had the extra X factor of spirit's help, which will make all the difference in wish fulfillment and magic.

Begin to breathe deeply and slowly in and out of your nose, relaxing more and more on each exhale. Today is a meeting day, a day of celebration, and a day of great transition for your energy and your magical abilities. There is a sense of excitement brewing as you step onto the stoop of the mansion of your soul. In the back gardens of the mansion is a party just for you. All of the spirit guides, spiritual helpers, angels, saints, sages, and beings of light are there waiting for you. You are the one they are waiting for. They want to show you how supported you are.

As you walk into the back gardens, see the smiles and feel the warmth in their eyes and the inspiration emanating from their very beings that is there to support you in your spiritual work and in your manifesting. You are ready. You have arrived at the juncture where you're living both with spirit and in the world. You can walk around and look at each of these beings of light that have been here cheering for you, wanting to show you how to direct your energy to help humanity make the next leap of consciousness in evolution where there will be more joy, love, compassion, and intuition.

As you are here in this place, notice how you're both sitting in physical space but also having a very real experience in spirit. You can always be with spirit, all the time. There is no separation. You can call on them to help you raise your frequency, shift your energy, and stay focused on loving-kindness all the time. They are here 24/7 to work with you and only help you see the truth of who you are and how much you can help the world through your own intention.

Feel connected to these spirit guides at your third eye, knowing they are not going anywhere. They are ready and willing to help you shift your life to live with pure love, excitement, and empowerment. They are going to help you manifest your next goal and are excited to be on this journey with you as your spirit team.

It is time to go back into the mansion of
your soul where you will break for now
from the meditation by taking three deep
breaths and coming back to the body.

Feeling the residue of the love from the party of your spirit
team, write down anything you noticed or that you would like
to remember in your journal. Take a break, maybe by going
for a walk, having a healthy snack, or playing in some way that
brings you into the present moment before continuing to the
next meditation.

Work with Your Spirit Guides to Help the World in the Way Your Soul Is Meant To

This is probably the meditation I am most excited to include in this book. The moment you decide to follow your soul purpose, everything shifts. You suddenly start to experience magic and see how easy it really is to manifest. Manifesting is much more powerful when our intention is pure and high vibration. Spirit guides are able to help you when your vibration stays in a positive state. Angels cannot really interfere with your life unless you ask, and all of the spirit beings that have evolved out of their physical incarnations exist solely to help humans who are answering the call to help the world evolve spiritually. You may be surprised, but you can start to experience interactions with life forms from other galaxies that live in other dimensions as you open yourself up to work with your spirit guides on your soul purpose.

Before this meditation, it would be wonderful to read your astrology birth chart, which you can look up online for free on websites like cafeastrology.com. If you use your time and location of birth, you can get some pretty in-depth information that can help you see your soul's natural strengths. This would lay the groundwork in your mental space for the true purpose of your soul to take root in the vision for your future. Even if you just read about your sun sign, you'll find quite a few big clues to your life purpose. You can also read about your life path number on totemrock.com by using their free life path calculator. The reason I recommend doing this is because the purpose of the soul is often phrased and looks different than what our mind conceives of as a purpose.

For example, we may have thought our purpose was about getting to a certain milestone in our life, which is about acquiring; however, the soul shows you how you can bring change to the world in a much more selfless way that will give you a deep will to use your energy for others. The language of astrology and numerology can help you start to think in these terms instead of the self-centered way of the ego and conditioned societal patterns of thought.

⁓

To begin the meditation, make sure you're sitting in a comfortable position with a straight spine. You may want to play meditation music and dim the lights to help get your body to relax. This is a big one and taking some time to make the space feel meditation friendly will help. Once you feel like you're ready to do this great awakening meditation, start to simply breathe in and out of your nose. Notice the breath and the quality of the breath that stands out. Is it warm, cool, energizing? Notice your body; is it holding tension anywhere? Can you instruct that area to let go with kindness?

You will now meet your higher self, who will take you to the guide who can help you see your soul's purpose. Your higher self will be waiting for you as your spirit guide takes you to a very high-vibrational realm of consciousness where there is pure peace, love, and wisdom. The space will feel as if it has been visited by spiritually evolved souls and those who have helped the world. The sense of humility is strong, as is the feeling of trust and dedication.

You will see before you a book that is your Akashic record. It holds the past, present, future, and your soul contract. In this book you can view your purpose. As you walk toward the book, see it begin to glow; your spirit guide is helping you be able to perceive this by holding your energy in the light with their loving friendship. Your guide can help you decipher what you see and understand what you are meant to know at this time. Just observe what you see when you look into the open book. Perhaps it's a vision, an image, a word, or something you don't yet know the meaning of.

Write down what you see and just tune into this for a little while, letting it sink in. See how it makes you feel and if there is anything more that comes to your awareness about this. The path will feel light, aligned, sure. You now know your purpose, and your guide is going to help you live it. Allow them to take you to a mountain now that overlooks many more mountains. They will bring up a vision of you living your purpose to help you see what to work toward. As they reveal this, it may surprise you. It may be something that has been in your heart all along.

Write down what you were shown and thank your guide for helping you align with this vision today. Take three deep breaths and slowly come back to where you're sitting.

~

Stay there for a little bit, integrating the meditation into your waking consciousness. How excited do you feel? Can you sense your soul beginning to flow through you? Congratulations on reaching this spiritual awareness and on opening your heart to perceive the purpose you incarnated for in this lifetime! Take a moment to write your purpose clearly, starting the sentence with "My soul's purpose is…"

Please do not despair if your purpose hasn't yet become clear. Sometimes spirit does not reveal something intentionally because it is lining up things to make it be delivered at the perfect time. Trust divine timing, and when you feel called to repeat the meditation, do. Also, often our purpose is multifaceted and we are shown parts of these facets when we are ready to perceive the type of purpose, which is frequently beyond the confines of our mind and much more energetic.

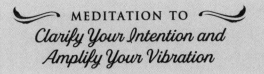

MEDITATION TO
Clarify Your Intention and Amplify Your Vibration

As you get used to manifesting with your spirit guides and their way of communicating, it is important to know that they help you in two main ways: clarifying your intention and amplifying your vibration. They may reveal ways that you can amplify your vibration by doing something different in your life or they may show you a feeling to focus on. They may help you by giving you something specific to focus on that will help you manifest it as well. If you're new to visualizing, they can help you hone your focus, really make it specific, so you can target your manifesting abilities at what you truly need to take the next step on your soul's journey.

This meditation will help you get specific with what you want to manifest next. Once you have that picture, you will charge your energy field to help you manifest it with the help of your spirit guide. If you were doing this without them, you wouldn't have the intelligence of a higher spiritual being to show you a new way of thinking that can create momentum in the etheric realms of creation they are familiar with. After all, they are already pure energy and have evolved out of the physical form.

Some human souls become so spiritually awakened that they join the realm of spirit guides to help the planet evolve from an energetic space that is far more powerful. Think of how easily people are swayed to spend money at Christmas without really rationally knowing why. Group consciousness is affected by energy, and that is the realm that spirit guides work to shift in order to alleviate fear, anger, and brutality from the face of the earth.

~

Begin the meditation by simply coming into your body through your breath. The body is the miraculous organic being that is alive because of spirit, and its presence is always moving through your organic body. The breath brings in the life force and each breath fills you with awareness. You're beginning to tune into this energy that is connecting you to the universe as you breathe deeply and slowly, relaxing and letting go.

You will now take some deep breaths to expand your aura and focus at your crown chakra to connect to your loving higher self. They will allow you to commune with your spirit guides in your usual place, and they will take you somewhere that will help you cleanse your energy field in the energetic realms. As they help you clear low vibrations from the storehouse of your consciousness, you sense that you're doing something that will actually make a real change in your life. You're prepping for the visioning they are going to help you with so you can manifest in the physical dimension. The feelings of shame, resentment, sadness, and disappointment are washed away as they help lift your vibration.

You will now sit on the top of a tall mountain and they will help you see exactly what you need to focus your energy on next for your journey. Perhaps it is a quality of being, a spiritual gift to work on, an act of self-love, a type of energy in your home, a move, a change, a resolution. Whatever physical or energetic thing they reveal is just fine. Just observe this and try to see the details, the colors, the temperatures, the sounds, the feelings of this goal. We often have many little steps in our journey, and this one is just as important as the ultimate goal.

Now see yourself having achieved this and see how you feel. Fill this vision with light and trust, knowing it will manifest. Feel the loving energy of the universe filling this vision because it is aligned to the greater good. Feel the power of your intention and the loving support of your spirit guides. You're doing great. The vision is now set in motion, and your intention is aligned to a very high-vibrational forcefield. Ask your spirit guide if they have anything else they want you to know, then just listen and observe. You do not need to control the message; just relax and wait. Write down if they had something to tell you and the vision you saw.

Thank your spirit guides and take three deep breaths, coming back to your body. Slowly return to waking consciousness.

～

You probably sense the energetic shift you've just made and will likely enjoy sitting in this energy. Write down anything else you'd like to remember or that stood out in the meditation.

MEDITATION TO
Help Manifest Things That Will Align You with Your Soul Purpose

Sometimes we need help to see the next step in our journey. Sometimes we just need to admit that we don't know where to start or how to get the ball rolling. However, spirit does and can help us when we ask. When you don't know what to ask for or it feels like the energy is stalled or blocked in your manifesting process, it's still important to work with your guides and ask them to send you what you don't know you need in your conscious mind. Being open to new opportunities, teachings, experiences, and blessings is an important part of manifesting.

Asking for help isn't always easy because it means giving up the idea of control. We want to control each step of the journey because it feels safe. Trust that spirit guides are working to help you step into a vision you may not even fully see yet. When you feel lost, this will help you stay in a high vibration. Continue to trust that things are working out as they should. This is a huge component in the manifesting process because, as the saying goes, "You can't always get what you want, but you get what you need." Often we are presented with a seemingly impossible situation because spirit is teaching us how to use our energy in a new way. A totally new awareness will often develop when we maintain our trust through confusion, blocks, and adversity.

Begin by focusing on your feet, specifically the bottom surface of your feet. Slowly bring your awareness up to the ankles, then the calves, knees, thighs, and to the hips. Taking slow and steady breaths in and out of your nose, bring your awareness up the spine to the base of the skull. Allow your awareness to move to the top of the head and remain just above the head. Envision a spiraling white energy going up from here as far as you can see. This energy connects you to another realm: the spiritual planes of existence where love is the means of communication.

Allow your consciousness to float up where you meet your spirit guide. Notice if this is the same guide or someone new. Notice if the way they show up surprises you or if you're easily able to accept their form and the way you perceive them. Feel the love they have for you and all of humanity as well as the wisdom that emanates from them. They will now take you to the mansion of your soul. Your higher self is there along with your spirit guide team and they are waiting for you.

It's time to ask for help. Humbly stand before the spirit world and admit you can't do it alone and you don't have all the answers. Tell them you want to live according to the highest good of all and that you need them to help you manifest the resources to do that. Feel their love emanating back to you as their energy kicks into gear working on your energy field to remove the lower vibrations. They are all ready at a moment's notice to start polishing your energy and raising your awareness. They may not deliver a solid idea of what action to take, but they will offer you an energetic antidote to your malaise. Let them help you shed the fear, the need to control, the need to have concrete knowledge of every step. Allow them to hold you and know that you're right where you need to be.

Before you leave, set your intention to stay open-hearted to the signs and blessings as they show up so that you can utilize them and step into your life's calling. With a smile, take your time as you leave the team working with you in this realm. Your spirit guide and your higher self know you've just opened to a new stream of energy that will greatly support you and shift your perception of reality. Take three deep breaths and return to the space you're sitting. Allow yourself to just notice how you feel and jot down anything that stood out.

～

In this chapter you've made great progress in your manifesting work. Think back to where your mind was when you read the first word on the first page of this chapter. You're growing more than you realize, and you're awakening much more than you think.

How to Further Develop
Your Work with Spirit Guides

*O*nce you have done the meditations in this book, it's likely that you will be very curious to open yourself to more ways of working with the spirit world. By far one of the most advanced ways of working with spirit guides is honing your ability to connect to the world of spirits that have crossed over from earth. This work has its own type of training and practice techniques but is just as possible as working with your spirit guides from other dimensions. Knowing that it is possible and requires a different approach can help you develop a very strong spiritual foundation that feels more grounded in the real world. By this, I mean that you will know it is not just your imagination and so will others.

I have studied with and seen very gifted mediums contact the spirits of the deceased, and each of these people have very active relationships with their own spirit guides. I truly feel that this ability to be a bridge to the deceased is one of the highest callings one can undergo as a human. The one thing that seems insurmountable in life is the end of life; yet a medium is able to show people that it is only the next step in the great journey.

The benefits that you will get from furthering your work with spirit guides to more advanced techniques are very rich and valuable. This journey does not lead to where we expect; we are conditioned to think it is some big house with a perfect spouse and potentially a very lucrative, well-positioned job in society. This work is about something much deeper, much more fulfilling, and bigger than any of us individually. Working deeper with your guides just means being willing to shed more layers of what you have thought life should look like in order to evolve your consciousness and be a part of the deep undercurrent of energy shifting humanity. It's a calling that requires great inner strength, wisdom, and trust that you get from the experiences you have working with spirit. It may mean you become very successful, but more than likely it means you will be guided to just the right places at just the right times to learn just the right lessons in order to be able to let go of the need to be seen as important.

This journey of working with your guides is something that you must take with them, but you can always ask for a spiritual healer to help you at any point in the journey. The process is one of diving deeper into your internal world and being able to establish boundaries, cut out toxic people, places, and things, and find your own way of being an energetic buffer in this world. Most of this work is internal and cannot be handed to you even in a book. I can, however, prepare you for a journey that will take many twists. This book will be a resource to return to when you feel confused so you don't lose hope in this beautiful journey.

Advanced work with spirit is an initiation into your higher-dimensional self. It puts you in the moments where you will be asked to decide what is moral, what is for the greater good, and what no longer serves humanity. It will help you find your strength and it will humble you. When trying to listen to spirit about why they asked me to include the topic of "advanced work," it became clear that this is likely not about you becoming a famous healer, author, actor, or politician. It is about you being perfectly content walking alone on your spiritual path. That is the greatest gift in life and one for which this book is a catalyst.

Often our spiritual work plucks us out of the role we were playing and eventually reinserts us into a much more humble means of existence where satisfaction comes from how we help the world and not from what we can get from the world. In many ways, it ends up grounding you right back into the world, so you relate to the pain of others and do not ignore it. It helps you show up for people instead of being callous and ignoring the suffering on the planet that is all around us. It often leads us to be more involved in our community, more dedicated to a life of service, and less addicted to the need to tell everyone what a good person we are. This advanced work might lead you away from the original spiritual groups you find yourself in sync with and even the first spiritual teachers you are drawn to. Our ego often takes years to shed, and at first we want to find power through our spiritual practice. Inevitably, over the course of possibly many lifetimes, we find ourselves able to be alone yet never alone.

Embracing the work of spirit often means coming up against something that seems insurmountable, being faced with great challenges, and feeling like you're being pushed to your limit. It means that you will be put in the places where you can grow the most and given the experiences that allow you to learn. It is not easy but it is rewarding, transformational, and leads to a profound sense of contentment with which you can face the world regardless of the challenge you are faced with. It also gives you an entirely new set of tools to tackle your challenges with so that you can overcome the impossible and thrive in the midst of chaos.

Spirit Circles and Working in Groups

Having kindred spirits to inspire you in your lifestyle of spiritual practice is, in my humble opinion, invaluable on this great journey. Their energy fields alone will help tune you into the spiritual realms. If you're new to having a daily meditation practice where you're able to contact spirits, joining a mediumship circle is a great way to make this something your nerves and your mind can do without so much resistance. These groups can be found on Meetup.com and by searching the internet for local groups. Often metaphysical centers, spiritual book stores, and spiritualists hold mediumship circles where the focus is solely on working with deceased spirits.

You can find meditation groups for different purposes, and it's important to know that one may be worlds different than another. It's also important to know that while some groups may have very grounded and stable people who have a spiritual lifestyle, other groups may be full of spiritual newbies who are struggling with their own morals and behaviors. Try not to let the people you encounter affect you too much. It's better to simply live more in your internal world of meditation than latch on too closely to these new spiritual friends. It is essential that you gather to be able to meditate, but do not confuse this new group as your new focus. The group energy is vital for everyone, but it can become more of a distraction and become something you replace an old friend circle with if you let it.

The good thing about doing meditation in a group is that you'll often find a very experienced and wise elder who can help you see your blind spot or answer questions that only someone with lots of knowledge can truly grasp. If you attend a more flashy group where it's a popularity contest, you'll find yourself falling back into old patterns of low-vibration thoughts, and that will be a key sign to find a more humble and experienced group. Approach groups with nonjudgment yet discernment. Allow your intuition to help you and tune into it frequently. There are many people who lack sound judgment in all places, just as there are many kind people in all places. Stay focused on the goal to enrich and open your inner life because it will be the rock in your life and the source of your happiness.

Introduction to the History and Practice of Seances

Spiritualism was started in the United States and is considered a religion. It is widely practiced in England, making it the eigthth most common religion in the country. It is based on the premise that the soul continues after death and that it can be proved by science. The practice of public demonstrations, circles in homes, and one-on-one sessions are all a part of the practices. In this spiritual practice, there are also manifestations of the spirits through ectoplasm and use of instruments that record disturbances in the energetic fields. Sometimes they listen for tapping and use ear trumpets.

Demonstrations of mediumship have been experienced across classes of people and across different cultures since its inception in the nineteenth century. The movement began in New York State and became the study of scientists trying to obtain evidence of the soul beyond death. As in many religions, there are some people considered frauds, but in my opinion, it is most important to educate yourself about the doctrines of any spiritual group and be informed about how their own group functions and know the good and bad of their history.

Embraced by the upper class, Spiritualism was a big part of Victorian English society. Demonstrations were hosted at the White House by Abraham Lincoln, the first woman to run for president in the 1800s was a spiritualist, and even Dan Aykroyd, who brought us *Ghostbusters,* is a fourth-generation spiritualist. The practice of spoon bending is often included in this study, which is one the most direct spiritual practices that shows the intersection of the physical world and the human psyche.

This religion is expounded upon in this book because it's important to know the history of practices within the spiritual community so you have a framework to understand the language and rhetoric, as well as a way to discern what direction will help you.

Evidential and Circumstantial Mediumship

Some people can have a hard time wrapping their head around the way that spirit guides communicate. Since they don't have a physical body, they convey ideas to your consciousness through images, sounds, words, and feelings. One way to ground your own experience of the spirit world and help others see that it is indeed very real even though you don't see it visibly (just like pheromones that get women's cycles synced) is through evidential mediumship. Working with the spirits of deceased loved ones is one way to work with spirit guides, as spirit guides can be a consciousness that used to be in a body. However, this type of work is like developing a whole different skill set because the frequency is different.

Circumstantial mediumship (which is common in the US) is where the person studies and practices inviting the spirit of a deceased loved one and then conveys the unresolved or important emotional messages of that loved one for whomever is requesting healing. The messages are often about unresolved situations or they simply share the type of personality of the deceased and help the person know their spirit lives on. Evidential mediumship (which is more common in the UK) picks up on facts such as the name of the street the person lived on, what they passed from, what their name was, etc. This can offer real closure for someone grieving because it is not vague and gives them proof of the other side. The difference between circumstantial and evidence-based mediumship is that one is subjective while the other is objective, i.e., qualitative versus quantitative.

If you plan to develop the skill of mediumship, your spirit guides will be your intermediaries in this process. You usually will have one guide that helps you work with spirits and helps you communicate with them. It's best to study mediumship with an experienced medium who can guide you in the process they work with to fine-tune their ability to read this dimension. However, having a strong connection with your guides will be a fantastic step toward that goal. Mediumship—as defined by most of the US as being the connection to deceased spirits—has tremendous potential to heal you and help assuage the heaviness of existential crisis.

If you have struggled with the exercises in this book because you're not used to this way of thinking and have a very active analytical brain, evidential mediumship may help you get over that hump. Seeing a well-respected evidential medium even over distance can help you start to overcome your own blocks to the spirit world's existence, which can have many layers. It can be an inspiring and life-changing event. As you continue to work with spirit guides, you may have deceased spirits show up because they are drawn to people with big open energy fields. You never have to work with them, and you can kindly tell them not now or not ever if you aren't open to trying to help them resolve an issue.

Usually spirits linked to a maternal lineage show up on the left and paternal show up on the right. In my (and others') experience, deceased spirits have a more dense vibration that is almost like a fog you can't see but can sense. The spirits hover lower in the air than non-human spirits, which are higher up. Friends are usually in the middle, and animal spirits are often lower to the floor. My teacher made it a point to only speak to one spirit at a time as they have a habit of piggybacking with like personalities and can speak together, confusing the messages. To further clarify this type of spirit guide work for yourself, I recommend a book called *Mediumship Mastery* by Stephen Hermann. Evidential mediums like Apryl Nicole and Eileen Davies are great to study with as well.

The magic of mediumship is that often a medium will reveal things to someone that they didn't know and can verify with another relative. This is one of the best ways to prove the spirit world is real.

Advanced Psychic Work and Resources

The Arthur Findlay College in England is one of the most highly regarded schools of mediumship in the world. One of their teachers, Eileen Davies, offers a private apprenticeship over the phone, which can be accessed by students around the world. To work with her, you likely will need to prepare yourself with much meditation, study, and practice. She determines whether working with a student is going to be a good fit on a case-by-case basis. You can also attend classes at the college or in her online classes. Other mediums such as Gordon Smith, Apryl Nicole, Afimaye Galarraga, and James Van Praagh also offer classes, and some have books and private sessions available.

If you're really feeling connected to this book and the words that I am catching from spirit as I write it, I would like to also guide you to a few books that may help further your study and development. One of the first books I read while going through my first major awakening was called *Synchronicity: The Bridge Between Matter and Mind* by David Peat. It really helped me see the world in a new way, and I believe it was a big energetic forklift in my ability to see beyond the veil of illusion, or separateness, that most people accept as all of reality.

Additionally, I would recommend reading more books about spirit guides from author Doreen Virtue. Her take on the spirit world comes through the lens of angels, which is inspiring and universal. Her experiences are often shared in her books as if you're on vacation with her, encountering spirits step-by-step while going about life in the real world. Her accounts were particularly life changing for me because she openly shared her own astonishment at finding spirit guiding her in the real world to a path of greater awakening.

Helping Others with Your Spirit Guides

Once you get used to working with your spirit guides, you can start to ask them for messages that would be helpful for your loved ones and friends. Even if you don't plan on being a professional healer, you will likely have people coming to you for advice when your frequency starts to shift. You can always check in with your guides to ask them if there is a friend who needs some support, and they will usually bring to mind someone that truly needs a friend at that time. You can even set your intention to the universe to let a friend you can help find you, and lo and behold, watch as they show up!

When you want to help someone with your own guides, the process is very similar to helping yourself. You want to be open and in a meditative state and ask open-ended questions. Your friend may be present or not, and your guides still can connect to how you may be able to help them. They often give advice that is simple, just as they do for you, and it will relate to energy instead of answers to yes-or-no questions.

If you want to help a family member or friend, though, they have to be open to it. You can always send them good energy, but you can't force them to believe you have a spiritual team of helpers that can change their life. We often have great excitement when our psychic abilities develop, and the first people we want to share the joy with are the ones we have deep bonds with. They may be open to a card reading or a loving conversation or they may not. You may be able to give them encouragement, a crystal, or a healing meditation soundtrack without going into detail about your guides. Not all souls are going to be open to the concept in this lifetime, and knowing that will help you sense where someone is and how to approach helping them.

Channeling in Written or Spoken Words

One of the big topics that inevitably comes up in the world of spirit guides is how we as an individual can share their loving messages, which can be so helpful for raising consciousness and offering healing perspectives in this world. Because we experience our guides in an energetic way through the chakra system and third eye, we can often allow the information to stream through writing. This can be information for you or for the collective that you can then share on social media or through channeling outlets. The process of channeling is a bit different for everyone. Many people like to approach it methodically by taking classes with a channeler who can help them with automatic writing or vocal channeling.

Personally, writing seemed to become a co-writing experience in most cases where my guides would help me have a newly expanded state of mind and ideas would flow through. There are instances where people are both conscious of being in an altered state and capturing the information that comes through as well as instances where people become an unconscious channel. It's important to talk about because it can be quite discombobulating if you are the unconscious channel type. Usually a guide will not force this and it's something you work toward, but as it was recorded in the case of well-known channeler Jach Pursel in the book *The Sacred Journey: You and Your Higher Self*, he was just a normal guy trying to meditate with his partner when he began to unconsciously channel Lazarus, his guide. He spoke and his partner recorded him, to his great surprise.

I have noticed a few things about connecting to higher-vibrational states that others have also confirmed. You get hot when your vibration raises. That's a clear sign you're making a connection. You'll often get chills with messages that are very important, and if you write to capture the thoughts/messages, you'll likely be writing very fast. Your vernacular may be different, and the rhythm may not be the way you usually write. When you're bringing through high-vibration concepts or ideas, it may even come through like a poem or a rhyme. Getting used to this type of communication is fun, and you can do it by setting the intention and going into meditation.

However, because I am not a vocal channel, I do not want to give advice on how to do that. The close friends and teachers I know that are vocal channels often begin to rock when they connect; this is nothing to be afraid of. Sometimes their voice changes to another accent or pitch and their energy field expands so much that walking in front of them will make them very nauseous. Are all vocal channelers legit? You will have your intuition to help you out on that question. If someone is using it for personal gain and not in a spiritual way, it likely is their own ego/imagination. If you can sense the energy shift and the intention is pure, you will likely know it is a real connection.

I just want to note that channeling is a voluntary act in almost every case I have heard of. Your intention to be a message delivery agent will help you.

Connecting to Someone Else's Guides

Another way to do healing work with guides is to connect to someone else's guides who may have important messages for them. This is one of my favorite ways to give a reading. I simply start the reading by setting the intention that our higher selves connect and bring through the messages that are most important for that person right now and then invite their spirit guides to also join us. Then I listen and see if I observe any specific guide or if a name comes to mind. Often it is easy to pick up on clients who connect to angelic energies, saints, and specific figures. The guides relay the message and I'd merely share it.

You really want to have the other person's permission if you're going to connect to their guides, and you also would likely want to practice offering readings before jumping to this style of reading. I started doing readings casually with oracle cards for friends and family for a few years before starting a clairvoyant development program. I think we each train in our unique way, and when you're ready, you will know.

One fun thing is that you'll find people who are open to the spirit world are easy to spot energetically. Their crown chakra will seem open, and they will have an imprint that matches other healers you know. I noticed this because when clients came in who gave me the impression of being a healer, they always ended up being one.

Basic Intuitive Sessions and Energy Healing

If you're feeling called to offer an intuitive session as a messenger for someone, you should feel excited, not intimidated. This is not about being perfect but about opening yourself to simply share the feelings you have openly with someone. I started by sitting down in front of my mom and sharing the feelings I felt that were reflections of hers. By reflecting them back to her, I was able to help her see what was weighing on her, and we came up with solutions to resolve it. After using cards for a while, I started by actually feeling what someone was feeling in their chakra system, which is called clairsentience. That was exhausting, and feeling everyone's stuff led me to develop a stronger relationship with my guides, and then I got the inspiration to connect to my client's guides. That made readings much easier physically, and I found their guides had specific insights for them that were very helpful.

In conclusion, if you'd like to use your connection to spirit guides to help others, start with cards or, if you're comfortable, a soul-to-soul conversation. Set the intention and know that you're naturally intuitive. Allow for the conversation to flow and don't try to impress or control the outcome. You can get a reading to see what they are like, and you can take classes. The more you jump into the spiritual community, the more comfortable you will feel. You don't have to feel like it is a competition of who is the most psychic because you will always be led to the person that you can help and vice versa. There is no power hierarchy in regards to healing. Even very experienced healers are going through the healing process day by day.

How to Add a New Type of Psychic Communication Ability Each Month

You may find that developing different types of psychic abilities allows you to receive messages from your spirit guides much more clearly. Just think about how much information we take in with all five of our senses. Take one away and we are missing out on a whole system of communication. It's the same in the spirit world. You can develop the different "clairs," which are different ways of sensing information in the spirit world. Here is a brief overview of each main type:

CLAIRVOYANCE is the ability to see images in your mind's eye in full color and receive information from these visions.

CLAIRAUDIENCE is the ability to hear words, songs, or sentences in your mind that are not coming from outside of your body but from spirit.

CLAIRSENTIENCE is the ability to feel a message through your own body and your chakras to be able to distill information for yourself and others.

CLAIRCOGNIZANCE is knowing information or having a gut feeling about someone, something, or an idea that you have no way of knowing except through your intuition.

CLAIRGUSTANCE is a more rare clair that involves getting tastes that give you clear messages from spirit and your intuition.

It would be far too difficult to try to work on all of these at the same time. It would be like trying to learn to play five new sports all at once. Try focusing on one per month and each day just tune into the intention to perceive information through this manner. Allow yourself time each day to observe through this sense for one month before moving on to the next skill in order to allow yourself the time to get used to this type of psychic sensing. For each person, the time it takes to open to a different clair will vary, so be patient with the process.

Put the type of psychic skill on a new vision board with each new moon and allow yourself a full two-and-a-half weeks of practice to see if the full moon brings you a new psychic ability. You'll really see how much progress you made after looking back over the course of a few months instead of trying to make it all happen instantly. Trust that when you ask the universe to help you manifest a new psychic communication ability and you consistently show up to work on it, it will show up! Read about each of the gifts as you're developing them to help yourself really turn your thoughts in the direction of that particular sensory perception. Just as an audio engineer starts to hear pitches others don't and an artist sees intricacies in lines others don't, immersing yourself into what you want to learn will allow your brain to support the learning process.

Shamanism

"Shaman" is a Siberian word for journeying into another dimension to contact spirit guides. A shaman is known as a spirit walker. They live as if they are split between the living and dead, the ancestors and nature. They are in tune with different life forms and communicate with the spirits of plants, animals, trees, weather, and earth itself. They can be of any gender and are deep listeners and wise wisdom keepers who live among all cultures.

Shamanism takes many different forms but often involves practices that induce a trancelike state, whether it's through drumming, dancing, or using plants. Not all shamans use hallucinogens to access the spirit world. In some cultures coffee is used, and in others sitting around a fire is a way to get into a meditative state. Shamanic initiations look different in different parts of the world. When one is interested in this path, it is usually because they are tuning into the spirits of nature, calling to them to help save them and the earth. The earth is being destroyed by consumer culture, and no one will be able to live in it if we do not shift our cultural ideologies to something more geocentric.

Many modern healers find their sole purpose is helping people come together to find empathy for the generations that are yet to come and find a spirit of activism through which we can restructure societal values to honor the very things that keep us alive like dirt, plants, water, air, and spirit. We are being called to step forward to help heal the planet in a very unique way. We are being asked to commune with the spirits of nature, who can remind us how to live in harmony with nature and guide us to take steps within our own communities to inspire earth-conscious living, whether it's reducing our use of plastic or finding ways to lower our carbon footprint.

There is a common occurrence reported among people who become shamans called the "shaman's sickness." This is often spirit's way of stopping you in your tracks, showing you how valuable it is to slow down in order to awaken you to your calling. This type of sickness is often your soul asking you to awaken to your true spiritual nature to unlearn the ways of modern society and walk a spiritual path that will help others find peace and healing. Not everyone will have a near-death experience that makes them suddenly change their life. For many, there is a nudge from their heart, an attraction toward nature- and earth-centered cultures. Shamanism has been practiced as far back as written history and is widely misunderstood as something that was based on superstition.

Much of the writings on shamans include an interesting facet about gender within this group. Often shamans are not ascribed to the gender roles of modern society. They often live solo or do not partake in matrimonial ritual. They relate to the common soul of humanity beyond the ideology of feminine and masculine role playing because they hear the whisper of spirits who say that the current cultural dominance of these ideas is hurting Mother Nature. Are we headed toward a gender-neutral culture where we are aware of ourselves beyond the confines of these roles? That is up to us. The world is just starting to see how gender roles have dominated the consciousness of modern humans, driving them to consume in an effort to fit into these roles. In a society where we can surpass these rituals, we can develop a meaningful system that allows for the proper care of nature and ourselves.

Specific Guides You May Cultivate Relationships With

There is no wrong approach to connecting to spirit guides, and while the majority of this book has focused on being open to the guide that shows up, many people find that intending to connect with a specific spiritual figure is very helpful. When we learn about spiritual figures or deities, sometimes we can use our connection to their story to help foster a connection. Additionally, connecting with guides that others have been connecting to for a long time gives us a Rolodex of sacred names through which we can heal and develop spiritually. It can also be argued that the more people that have prayed to a specific figure, the more open the channel and stronger the group consciousness is that can help you access them. There is nothing wrong with choosing a spirit guide to try connecting to, and it can greatly enhance your team of spirit guides. This mode of connecting to the spirit world is direct, commonly practiced, and gives people great results!

Here is a non-exhaustive list of spiritual figures you may find call to you, and I encourage you to also explore more. Some of these figures lived in human form and some likely did not. I also included star systems, which are groups of consciousness that you may find it helpful to work with, as many others have.

Please keep in mind that each of these figures has a rich history that you may find it helpful to read more about. Each unique culture has long-standing traditional ways of contacting their spiritual figures, and looking more into those practices would also likely be helpful. Getting in tune with a deity starts with intention, and taking certain actions should always be done reverently, honoring the many generations of holy women and men who have guarded the practices so they can be passed on.

Egyptian

Isis: Seen as the mother goddess of ancient Egypt, she has powerful magic that can be called upon. She was said to have resurrected her lover Osiris from the dead and was the mother of Horus. She is known for her wisdom, healing, and great magical abilities.

Connecting to her energy calls upon the divine feminine, which allows you to manifest. Working with her directly can help you find your ability to help heal others as she healed her son Horus. As a mother to all pharaohs in a spiritual sense, she can be called upon to bring out your nobility and leadership abilities to help the world. If you're seeking to find your own sense of maturity, power, and spirituality, perhaps this goddess is calling to you.

THOTH: Known as the scribe of Ra, Thoth is the keeper of divine records and can create magic through the power of words. Thoth is a powerful god who helps people harness their communication skills (such as writing) and share their love through creative expression. He was also an advisor to the gods, linked to the intuitive wisdom of the moon, and can be worked with when you yourself are trying to find your way on your spiritual path and make life changes. He can help you learn about the unseen realms and other dimensions, which makes him a great teacher and spirit guide. If you're looking to rewrite your story to something that allows you to co-create the reality you want instead of living in fear, calling on his energy can help you find the right perspective.

Celtic

BRIGHID: Known as the goddess of the home, she is most widely seen as a powerful deity of prophecy.

If you're trying to bring in a happy home life, hone your intuition, or read energy, the fire energy of this goddess is one to call upon. Her fire can help with songwriting, poetry, healing, and magical manifesting goals. She is known to help one perfect a craft and find excellence by becoming highly intelligent. If you're looking to expand in your career of healing or creative pursuits, she can help you become greatly skilled in your craft. All Celtic deities are connected to the land, and her energy connects to highlands, hills, and rising fire, which may help you to forge a relationship with her. She helps women find their power and helps with both fertility and new growth. Building a relationship with her can help in scholarly pursuits, family life, creativity, and healing.

DAGDA: The father god of Ireland has long been called upon for abundance. Abundance doesn't have to be just money; it can be food, friendships, goodness, and positivity. He is known as a good god who oversaw the supply of food and made sure there was enough. If you find yourself fearful that you won't be able to make ends meet or feel you are blocked in any way by fear, call on his good nature to help you see that you always have enough. He is also able to help you start out on new ventures and discover new knowledge that will help you succeed. If you feel like others seem to have an easier time attracting what they need and desire living a rich and full life, balanced with love and the things that make life comfortable, perhaps working with Dagda is the perfect next step. Placing a cauldron or phallus image or statue can help you connect to this energy.

Greek

APHRODITE: Aphrodite was known as a goddess of sexuality that arrived when Uranus was castrated. She was married but took many lovers without shame. She is called upon when one wishes to open to passion, romance, and find their own seductive qualities. If one is trying to overcome shame, feel more beautiful, or accept their desires more fully, she is a great guide to work with. She can be connected to by eating aphrodisiacs such as lavender, chocolate, and shrimp. If you feel like your love life is nonexistent, not exciting, or really routine, she could be a great goddess to work with to find your spark once again and know that it comes from the energy within you and not from someone else.

HERCULES: This demigod was half human and endured many struggles. He was the son of Zeus, and during his major struggles he was able to use his divine half to overcome them. He was able to find superhuman abilities and not be destroyed by difficulties because of his spiritual strength. He is a guide to look to when you need great endurance and spiritual anchoring. Many of us go through hardships at different points in our lives and must find our spiritual foundation to stay calm during chaotic times. Herculean energy is great to connect to when you feel you're being tested, are suffering from loss or pain or circumstances that are out of your control. The strength of Hercules is now a frequency you can call upon for divine spiritual connection to find that your life may seem to be falling apart, but you can still feel all right within your soul.

Yoruba

OBATALA: As one of the seven African powers, he is known as the creator of life. He is often called upon to bring more peace and harmony into one's life. He is known to help open you to creative energy, which can allow you to see more solutions to your problem. The purity of his energy can help you find your own pure intentions, which allows you to perceive new possibilities and see through the lens of compassion, tolerance, and possibility. His color is white. You can create an altar to connect with him using coconut, rice, and white yams. He can help you find peace in relationships, establish justice in your life, and find your own sense of leadership.

OSHUN: This orisha is called upon for fertility, abundance, finding employment, and getting things to flow in your life. She is often honored by placing a bowl of river water on an altar and connects through the crystals amber and coral. Hers is a motherly energy that is honored every August with the annual Oshun festival. She has her own altar in Nigeria that people visit throughout the year and is a designated

UNESCO World Heritage site. Her story includes offering protection to those who prayed to her when they were under siege. If you want to find your sensuality, protect your energy from those who mean you harm, and find more blessings, connect to Oshun. Her colors are yellow and gold.

Archangels

CHAMUEL: This archangel is one that can help you find peace in your relationships. In sacred texts this angel was said to have provided comfort and relief in times of great turmoil. He is associated with the color pink and can help you find healing after heartbreak or betrayal. He is often worked with when someone has had relationship trauma and is also the go-to angel that can help you find lost objects. The symbol of this archangel is usually a heart because of how he helps you feel peace in your heart. He can help you forgive, work through things, and develop healthy relationships with others. If you want more wisdom to face your interactions and smooth things out with people, this is a great relationship to cultivate.

RAPHAEL: Also known as St. Raphael, his name means "he who heals." He is an archangel that is called upon for physical healing and comes to you right away, no matter what. He is often associated with the color of dark green, and using crystals that color or incorporating those colors onto your altar may help forge a relationship with him. Raphael can help you work on the energetic layers of healing and can help you when you want to pray for the healing of someone else. He can help you by raising your vibration to alleviate stress that may be contributing to poor health or feeling uneasy. He is of the highest order of angels and has great energy that people often feel in a very real sense.

Ascended Masters

MELCHIZEDEK: Mentioned in the Bible, this figure lived on the earth and became an ascended master without dying. This spiritual figure is said to oversee the transmutation of energy on the planet by helping those spiritual seekers who commit to raising the planetary frequency. It is said that Jesus was of the order of Melchizedek and that he is a very high-dimensional being now. He is often channeled through highly developed spiritual figureheads who have the ability to match his frequency and share his visions for a better, more peaceful world. This enigmatic figure can help if you are trying to find the courage to live the path of your soul, and he can also help you find a balance between your spiritual life and being within the physical world.

METATRON: Known as the overseer of the creative blueprint, this figure is said to hold a cube of sacred geometry that is passed over energy to give it form. Metatron is said to sit next to the Divine and can help us plug into our own ability to manifest through pure intentions. He is often considered an overseer in the angelic realms and depicted at the top of the Tree of Life. As the figure who oversees the sacred codes that create harmony and life, he can be worked with to download art, ideas, and energy that can be implemented through your actions to help shift the planet to a more evolved state. The grids of sacred geometry can be accessed when you set your intention to work with this spirit guide, and you will be opened to great wisdom.

Saints and Prophets

ST. CHRISTOPHER: The patron saint of travelers was said to have lived until the year 251. He is called upon for protection from sudden death and accidents. During his life he devoted himself to helping people cross a very dangerous river and was said to have been visited by Christ in the form of a child wherein he was tested. As he helped the child, the waters rose and the child became heavy. St. Christopher, who was said to be very tall, was able to help the child to safety. This story has endured, showing that the weight of the world can be lifted with high-vibration energy to serve the greater good for all. If you feel you would like to be supported on your journey in a spiritual way and be protected from distractions on your spiritual path, call on this spirit guide.

ST. FRANCIS OF ASSISI: St. Francis lived until the year 1226 as a Catholic monk. As a brother of the order, he inspired the entire lineage of Franciscan monks. He inspired others to give up their material possessions and live a life of compassion. He would commune with nature often and is considered the patron saint of ecology. He is called upon by those who wish to quell their desires of the ego as he himself did after a life of partying. He heard God in a dream call him to begin his work in the church and underwent much public disdain for his decision to forgo a luxurious life of fame and fortune. If you're looking for deeper meaning in your life and need someone to help you find the courage to walk away from modern living habits that keep you stuck in your own ego, seeking material and societal status, call on this spirit guide for energetic support. Just as St. Francis listened to his spirit guide in a dream, he also experienced the divine in person as a leper who showed him respect when he acknowledged him. St. Francis can help you see creation as an interconnected, interdependent web and live from a place of valuing people for their soul and not their looks.

JESUS: Known as a ninth-dimensional being in the realm of ascended masters, the teachings of Jesus have been written over and over for thousands of years as language and politics changed. The string of truth within the teachings continues to pull people away from misery and into trust that love can save the world. If you want to find the true energy of Christ, try connecting to him directly in meditation just as you would with any other ascended master. You may find that messages are much more simple than the parables in the Bible, which are influenced by their writers and the politics of the time they were written. Jesus can help you forgive others and yourself and find "the kingdom of heaven" that is within you.

MOTHER MARY: Mary was said to have been visited by the angel Gabriel and told she would have a son. The holy spirit is also said to have told her she would be the Mother of God. She is seen as a pure spirit who is able to help us find our own purity, which many people often associate with virginity. Most accept that she lived on this earth and experienced her own guides who foretold her future before she became a spirit helping us from the other side. For those who have trouble rectifying their religion with that of spirit guides, this is the perfect spiritual figure to work with. She also helps with healing and finding a divine connection, and she can be called on to feel nurtured. Additionally, she can help those struggling to see their value as a woman to celebrate their own divine nature.

Buddhist

BUDDHA: *Buddha* means "enlightened one," and in Mahayana Buddhism there are five celestial beings that live in the spiritual realms. The man historians believe to be the original Buddha, Siddhartha Gautama, left a lineage of peace that has endured for thousands of years. To connect with the Buddha, you can practice meditative walking, sitting, or breathing, as well as read the Buddha's teachings. There are beautiful statues and art that are considered "zen" and help one connect to the mind of the Buddha, which now contains the consciousness of many that have attained enlightenment. If you are wishing to face life with a sense of joy and embrace suffering with acceptance, connecting to the Buddha would be a great spirit guide resource for you.

TARA: Known as the goddess of compassion, Tara is often subdivided into the Green or White Tara. Green Tara represents the night, and White Tara represents the day. She strives to uphold humanity by inspiring enlightened actions to end suffering. She is often called upon for protection while traveling and assistance on the path to enlightenment. She is the most widely regarded deity of Tibet, and the mantra that calls upon her can be used to connect to her energy: *Om tare tuttare ture svaha.* The origins of her story can also be traced back to the goddess Parvati of Hinduism. For those wishing to infuse their own consciousness with serenity and compassion to engage with the world through peaceful action, she is a wonderful spirit guide to build a relationship with.

Yogic

BABAJI: Also known as Mahavatar Babaji, he is said to reside etherically in the Himalayan Mountains, appearing to students and initiates of Kriya yoga.

He was the teacher of Lahiri Mahasaya, and many yogic lineages trace back to these teachers. He is often depicted wearing a loincloth and has a bluish tint due to the herbs that yogis lived on in the caves. He has been reported to come to those who wish to cleanse their body and mind energetically through the practice of yoga for the purposes of spiritual enlightenment, and if you're seeking a deeper path of yoga, he would be a great spirit guide to call upon. Reading books that account others' experiences of him can help, and *Autobiography of a Yogi* is a great place to start.

Paramahansa Yogananda: This yogi, considered a saint to many, was alive from 1893 to 1952. He is considered one of the fathers of modern yoga in the West and was himself guided by his own spirit guides, as depicted in his book *Autobiography of a Yogi*. He founded the Self-Realization Fellowship after being visited by Jesus and told to help people find God through meditation in the West. He met many saints in his travels to India who had supernatural abilities and was able to fulfill his soul's calling to establish a strong lineage of spiritual practice. If you're looking to find a spiritual connection without having to follow one person, his energy is very pure and non-egoistic, and he can help you find spirituality beyond dogmatic practices.

Taoist

THE DRAGON KING: Dragons are said to live in the waters, and the Dragon King—which is divided into four beings who live in the four directional oceans—is highly venerated. The Dragon King is a benevolent god whose mood can be seen through the weather and water movement. He has a long history of being able to help provide rain when needed to help produce food. If you feel called to work with the Dragon King, research more into his history among the Chinese culture and you'll find there are many strengths to call upon him for, including that of spiritual awakening. Often exploring a culture that is new to you can help you develop the ability to see beyond differences and the strength of forging peace and meditation. Dragons are also great to work with for wealth and fortune.

WHITE TIGER: This figure is a protector and can be called on to keep negative energy away, even if it's in your own thoughts. The tiger is one of the major Chinese figures and is able to help you find your destiny. There are many books written on the white tiger as a part of the rites of passage one goes through on the path to enlightenment. If you're looking to sustain a spiritual path and feel strong even when you feel alone in your endeavor, this is a spirit guide to work with. A tiger is strategic, aware of its surroundings, and strong and fierce. If those qualities are something you'd like to procure, this is a good guide for you as well.

Hindu

GANESHA: Ganesha is one of the most highly regarded and auspicious deities in the Hindu religion. He is often depicted as a man with an elephant head riding on a mouse and is known as the remover of obstacles. This can help you if you feel stuck in any area of your life, even if you don't know the direction you want to go. If you feel there are insurmountable obstacles or that you're between a rock and a hard place, call on Ganesha to help you find a way through. Ganesha can help you shift your perspective and is a great god to call on for luck and fortune as well. As the patron deity of authors and intellectuals, he can offer wisdom, patience, and peace.

KALI: This goddess, the embodiment of Parvati, wife of Shiva, is often depicted with her tongue out or holding a head. She was said to have slayed the demon from which all others were born. As the goddess of death and darkness, she is called upon at the new moon to help us experience a letting go of old consciousness so we may be reborn into the light. She embodies Shakti energy, which is the divine feminine and creative force of the universe. She is often called upon for creativity and sexuality, and she allows you to face your own darkness/shadow courageously in order to find your power.

Star Systems

ARCTURIAN: The planet that orbits the star Arcturus is said to be the home of this advanced civilization that works collectively and telepathically as a united consciousness of love. This civilization works to help throughout the universe where others are trying to combat lower vibrations. They help our group consciousness prepare for progress and allow us to make evolutionary leaps through the relationships they forge with us telepathically. They are kind, benevolent, and in higher dimensions than what most humans are able to perceive if they have not activated their upper chakras. If you feel called to help humanity shift, you may feel called to read more or meditate on the starseeds on the planet from Arcturia, which can link with your consciousness and help you see from an elevated perspective.

PLEIADES: A group of beings from a more advanced civilization that can communicate telepathically. They have contacted spiritual adepts on Earth and are said to help us with our ascension process out of pure care and concern for the future of our planet. They have been publicized through various sources as coming with intentions to help raise planetary frequency. This star system can be seen in the sky, and many indigo children feel an affinity for one or more star systems as if they remember them or have lived there before. Relating to the Pleiadians is not new in human history. Many Native Americans believe they come from this star system as starseeds to help bring light to this planet. If you feel drawn to work with this group, reading Barbara Hand Clow's *The Pleiadian Agenda* may be a nice point of entry.

Conclusion

𝒰ltimately, our connection to spirit guides helps us do one thing: leave this planet better than when we found it. Spirit guides show us how to think about the connection of all of life and sense the joy available to us when we live for the greater good. Whether our guides allow us to be a happier, more peaceful person or they guide us to a job that helps change the world, anything we do to become more loving, peaceful beings is a positive impact. Your guides are ready and waiting to work with you and show you that you can be peaceful and contribute to the utopia that all of humanity is evolving toward together.

If you face a relationship or situation where you find it hard to share your enthusiasm for spirit guides, try to just continue to have that relationship without losing the connection you've worked so hard to build. You do not have to cut ties with people who do not believe in the spirit world just because you start to see this reality. You also don't have to change their minds. You can focus on your own energy and still do a lot of good in the world.

Spirit guides help us all find compassion and tolerance for where each soul is on their journey, knowing we are experiencing parts of ourselves that are trying to learn and find their way back home to the ultimate oneness of love. In a world that seems to be more and more separated by ideologies that spark division, spirit guides offer us a language and a method to overcome divisive thinking. Spirit guides show us universal truths: we all need love, crave community, and make mistakes. Spirit guides show us how to forgive ourselves and others, and they lead us to the light when all we see is darkness. Spirit guides, in my humble opinion, are one part of the solution to war, hunger, and inequalities on this planet. The more of us who experience and cultivate this relationship and know how helpful it is, the better it will be for our children and our children's children.

The next time you sit down to connect and work with your spirit guides, remember that this sacred connection is bigger than you, and it's helping you see the world through the eyes of wisdom, which will help spread love.

APPENDIX

Meditation Tool Guide

~ Crystals ~

Use this section to select crystals that will help you connect with your guides. Crystals have been great allies, treasured by many groups throughout history for their mystical properties. They help raise our vibrations to reach spiritual realms and release lower vibrations that keep us from feeling the love and inspiration available to us from our spirit guides. The various properties associated with each crystal are from observations made over time by sensitive healers, but there is no hard and fast rule about what to use each crystal for. If you feel called to use a particular crystal, you will certainly find your best allies by listening to which ones seem to be calling to you.

Crystals to Connect with Angels

ANGELITE: This pale blue stone works on your throat chakra, opening up a channel of communication between you and the spirit world. It is known to help alleviate anxiety and connect you to the angelic realm, which offers you unconditional love and support. It can help you find a state of peace and relieve stress. It can help you deal with anger, and it opens the upper chakras, which aid in your overall connection to your spirit guides. It sometimes has white in it too, which indicates it can be helpful in creating a bridge at the crown chakra, which is the gateway to the spirit realms. This calming energy can help you recover and heal from trauma or burnout by helping your thyroid and balancing your energy levels. It gets its name from its tremendous ability to help you connect to the angelic realm, which is waiting to help you.

SERAPHINITE: This green crystal has little silvery slashes in it, making it luminescent, and it appears to have little angel wings in it. It does many things to help your energy field such as clear the aura and help balance the chakras. This crystal is particularly helpful for the nerves as it helps rebalance the energy and re-create a sense of balance and well-being. It can help one break negative cyclic thoughts to help raise your vibration and encourage you to connect with your spiritual allies. It has been known to help bring in the energy of archangels specifically. Use this crystal to call upon the archangels and assist you in healing, creating a positive energy field, and breaking patterns that are hurtful to you in your thoughts. This crystal is known to help connect to nature spirits as well. Because of its green color, it is wonderful for heart chakra healing. This crystal may help you hear messages from angels clairaudiently. It is said to carry the divine feminine energy and may be used to connect with goddess energy.

Crystals to Connect with Ancestors

MOOKAITE: This jasper is a beautiful combination of yellow, red, pink, purple, orange, white, and brown. No other crystal appears this way, indicating its unique ability to help you heal in specific areas. This crystal has been known to help people heal from

ancestral karma and past lives. It can help you find
your sense of a spiritual self and detect the vibration of
your unique soul. It can help you recognize and clear
genetic patterns that are stored in your energy field.
Australian Aboriginals use this crystal in healing,
and it gets its name from Mooka Creek, where it is
found. Because much ancestral connection is done
to understand the energy we still carry with us, this
crystal is your ally to help you to find freedom from
the actions and perspectives you inherited that may
be lowering your vibration. The red of the crystal can
help you feel connected to the earth for clarity in your
meditation work.

SHATTUCKITE: This crystal is a vibrant blue with
turquoise and purple. Known to be a crystal that can
help you connect with extraterrestrials, it also can help
telepathic connection to your ancestors. It helps open
the channel of communication at the throat chakra as
well as stimulate the third eye. This is the crystal most
well known to help with connection to deceased loved
ones and mediumship. It enhances psychic abilities
and is known to open the connection to spirit guides.
Because it also has protective qualities, it will help you
connect to spirit guides that work in the light and
are evolved spiritual beings. This stone can help you
use your own words to create in a loving and inspired
manner. As all our words create vibrations, you can use
this to set the intention to live in constant connection
with your higher self and guides throughout the day.

Crystals to Connect with Celtic/Druid Deities

BLOODSTONE: This green and red crystal is linked to the Celtic goddess Brighid. It is said to have been used by athletes of ancient Greece for strength and stamina and was even worn in battle to stop bleeding. The stone can help you detox from negative energy and is protective and grounding. It targets both the heart and root chakras to help you feel grounded and lead to growth. It also has been known to bring luck. This is one of the most prominent crystals for physical healing, and it has been used throughout history to help with wound healing and circulation. It has been linked to fertility and is sometimes used for menopause and PMS. The crystal can be used to call upon your own ability to self-heal. You may find it helps you connect to other spirits in the Celtic, Roman, or Greek traditions. If you find yourself in negative environments, this is a great crystal to work with to keep your vibration higher so you can stay connected to the spirit realm.

MERLINITE: This crystal is a unique blend of black and white with hues of gray and blue. It sometimes appears as though a black plant is growing within it. The crystal, which comes from New Mexico, is said to help in connection to spirit guides as well as wizard energy such as that of Merlin, which is how it gets its name. If you would like to work with your guides on healing your shadow, this crystal is helpful in finding the power within your own darker aspects. It is great for enhancing psychic abilities and can help you reclaim your power to help you manifest. If you're interested in magic, this is the perfect crystal to work with as it helps you find the balance between push and pull or yin and yang with the universe and yourself. It can also help you connect to a number of gods and goddesses who have been known to have great power and can be helpful allies in working magic. If you're ready to do spiritual work on yourself, this crystal can be a catalyst for you.

Crystals to Connect with Buddha

JADE: This crystal has two distinct variations that are usually green. It has been used traditionally in Buddhist cultures to promote harmony, longevity, and a peaceful death. Sometimes called the friendship stone, it also promotes healing and can help reduce anxiety. It may be used when someone has been through a shock to help them find a sense of calm. It is used to attract luck and bring wisdom of your true self. A crystal with much to offer, you can use jade to connect to a state of balance and health in mind, body, and spirit in order to achieve deeper meditative states. If you are pessimistic, this can help you change your attitude or overcome a victim mentality. Jade is known to help promote beauty and give the wearer more energy. This can help protect your energy and bring peace so your mind will become still. This crystal works on the largest energy center, the heart chakra, which is what extends outward and senses energy, picking up other people's pain. This is good to use if you feel overwhelmed with empathic pain.

Rose Quartz: This pink crystal is another crystal that is often associated with the tradition of Buddhism and used by monks. As it helps heal the heart chakra, it promotes self-love and healing. It has a calming and soothing effect that will help you connect to the upper chakras in order to sense your divine teachers. This is a great stone to help you release old pain that may be weighing you down or distracting your mind in meditation. It is used in Buddhist traditions because, like jade, it promotes the feelings that the Buddha teaches one to cultivate such as peace, harmony, and unconditional love. Also like jade, it promotes friendships and can help restore relationships or even attract new ones. This crystal is often used to help one attract love and can be used to connect with other spirit guides as well. Because of its pink color, it is also associated with the crown chakra, which is the gateway to the spirit world. It has also been used to connect with the Chinese goddess Quan Yin, the goddess of compassion.

Crystals to Connect with Ascended Masters

Celestite: This icy blue crystal is known to help the brain, eyes, ears, mouth, throat, and nose. It is a combination of the colors of the throat and crown chakras, making it a great crystal for communicating with high-vibration guides. Its purifying effect on the physical and energetic bodies will help you feel at ease and peaceful for meditation. It is known as one of the highest vibration crystals that can aid in reaching the spirit realm. It can help you learn about the spirit world as well as lower anxiety. It is a great crystal ally to work with if you want to be a healer or learn how to help others. Often when you are trying to open your spiritual connection to your divine teachers, this crystal will just call to you. Its luminescent quality will help you find the emotional energy that matches its bright sheen. It is also used to help reduce pain, attract love, stop racing thoughts, and restore relationships. It is a great crystal to wear to stay connected to the spirit world throughout the day and induce a creative state. This connects to the divine feminine energy and would be helpful in connecting to goddesses as well as ascended masters.

SELENITE: This white crystal is often used to help clear other crystals as it is so powerful. It is known as the clearing crystal because it helps cleanse your energy field. It helps clear all the chakras and especially helps open the crown chakra. It can help improve the spinal column and is often placed in offices to help the energy remain positive. It is a wonderful crystal to use to connect to ascended masters as it helps raise your vibration to be able to match these high-level beings. It will give you clarity and calmness as you meditate with it. It greatly enhances intuition as it removes negative energy from the aura. This crystal can be waved around the body to help clear positive ionic buildup from electronics, and it can help restore harmony in the physical body. It is known as one of the most popular crystals for connecting to the spirit realm and helping you with spiritual transformation. People often use this to call on protection from angels and connect to ascended masters such as Christ and Metatron.

Crystals to Help Activate Spirit Communication

APOPHYLLITE: This clear or greenish cluster of pyramids is an excellent bridge to use in meditation in order to contact spirit guides. It is known to help open the third eye and ease anxiety. It has a very high vibration and is commonly used to contact the angelic realms. Because it helps your aura by raising your vibration, you will find it easier to meditate when you're holding this crystal. This crystal is probably best known for being the best at raising the kundalini energy stored at the base of the spine, which opens one to enlightenment. If you find your mind going too quickly when you're meditating, this crystal will help calm your mind and body to help you connect with your guides. If you find yourself constantly thinking about your finances, relationships, or feeling like you can't use your imagination, this is the perfect crystal to help shift those energies by moving energy from the lower chakras to the upper chakras.

LAPIS LAZULI: This blue stone has specks of yellow and looks like a starry night. It was originally found in Afghanistan and has been highly valued as a crystal to connect with the gods by both the Egyptians and Sumerians. It is used to aid in the activation of the throat chakra and has tremendous healing properties. It is known to help your immune system, aid in sleep, and clear karmic energy that causes illness, and it is known for many more physical healing properties. It can help you feel and express a strong sense of self. By aiding in an expanded viewpoint, you can ask this crystal to help you heal yourself and see your own energetic patterns. This bridge-building crystal is the perfect way to start working with energy and connecting to the spirit world. It is a strong amplifier for your self-esteem, which can help alleviate low vibrations and foster quicker connections to your spirit guides.

Crystals to Connect to the Faery Realm

FAIRY QUARTZ (ALSO KNOWN AS SPIRIT QUARTZ): Often a beautiful lilac color, this crystal has many little pyramid points on it. Each of the little crystals amplify each other, making it very powerful. It helps you integrate your spiritual self into your life and is known to help you become more aware of spirits and their unconditional love for you. You will feel more uplifted and expanded with this powerful crystal. Coming from South Africa, this crystal is mined by women. Its white, pink, and purple colors help activate the upper three chakras as well as the eighth chakra, or aura. This crystal can help connect to the etheric and sparkly realm of faery beings as well as other high-vibrational spiritual guides. You may find that this crystal's vibration can help you overcome blocks in your meditation process as it has a very unique and noticeable energy.

PERIDOT: This green crystal is one that can help you connect to your guides in your dreamstate and is known to help connect to the faery realm. Faeries are known to hang out around plants, and this crystal has the same color of plants, making it attractive to these spirits. The playfulness of the faeries is also attracted to the energy of this stone, which brings about a sense of cheerfulness. It will help you release and let go of low-vibration emotions such as jealousy, resentment, and frustration so you can be more present and sense the energy around you, where the faeries are waiting to make contact with you. Try holding the crystal and calling upon the faeries to connect to your energy field.

Crystals to Open the Crown Chakra

MOONSTONE: This white, milky crystal is somewhat transparent, with a bluish and sometimes rainbow sheen to it. It is known to help physical health as well as emotional stability. It is a very popular crystal for enhancing psychic abilities as it resonates with the crown chakra. Its calming energy can help you overcome the block that strong emotions have in your meditations. It is known to help calm issues related to a blocked crown chakra such as insomnia, hair falling out, or rashes. It also helps one develop a stable connection to the spirit world without too much energy concentrating at the crown chakra, which can lead to feeling ungrounded. Some crystals raise the energy so quickly that it can feel like being caffeinated, but this crystal offers a gentle approach to self-transformation and a protective energy while you sleep.

SCOLECITE: This crystal is usually white with bright white lines in it. It is one that you can feel the energy of when you hold it, and because of its pure white color, it can help you open and activate the crown chakra, which also vibrates with the frequency of the color white. This interdimensional crystal can make you feel a loving bond between you and your higher self and is a great crystal to use while working on developing that connection. The crystal is often used to aid in sleep and lucid dreaming, but it can have the same effect in meditation. If you feel like you're too focused on the negative, this will help you develop a sense of gratitude while giving you a sense of being safe and content. This is the perfect crystal for both beginners and experienced meditators looking to connect to the spirit world.

Crystals to Open the Third Eye

AMETHYST: This purple crystal works on all the chakras to help balance them, but it is most commonly used to enhance the function of the third eye chakra. It has many helpful benefits for physical health such as calming the heart and nerves and even sometimes helping reduce headaches and heartburn. It's known to help the immune system as well. As a powerful transmuter of negative energy, it will bring more positive energy into your aura. It is a great crystal to use when you want to open yourself to clairvoyance as it can help you start to see images in the mind's eye. In ancient Greece it was said that cups made of amethyst were used to protect against drunkenness. This is most likely the most popular of all crystals for its well-known ability to enhance psychic abilities and reduce anxiety. This crystal is great to use if you feel like you need to improve your memory or want mental clarity. It can help you heal and is also wonderful to use if you're dealing with anger, grief, or sadness.

CHAROITE: This purple crystal often has white or black in it and is used to help you stop an overactive mind to enhance your ability to just receive information from the third eye without the mind getting in the way. This crystal can help you see your own energy more clearly so that you can release self-sabotaging thought and behavior patterns. It will help you feel the unconditional love and connection to spiritual energy that can help you face the biggest fears such as the fear of death. If you need to get out of toxic situations that you create for yourself, this can help you rely on your spiritual connection to know you can shift your life and trust that everything will be okay. This is one of the crystals that is known as a teacher or guide because it helps you with decision-making.

Essential Oils

Essential oils are a powerful meditation tool to help deepen your connection to your guides. Not all essential oils are safe to ingest or use topically. Be sure to follow the specific usage instructions for each oil you procure.

AMBER: If you want to work with your guides on attracting abundance, this is an oil that will help you get into the frequency that attracts success and good fortune. It will help you connect to guides that can help amplify your magnetism and lower stress.

CEDARWOOD: This grounding, woodsy oil can help you center your energy if your mind is all over the place. It is often used to connect to Celtic deities as well as aid in manifestation. It can help you feel safe as it helps your root chakra.

EUCALYPTUS: This invigorating herb helps the heart, throat, and third eye chakras as it helps respiratory and nasal passageways. It is good to use if you're holding a lot of emotional baggage from past experiences that may be lowering your energy and affecting your meditation. This clearing oil is great to use regularly to keep yourself refreshed energetically.

GERANIUM: If you want to work with your guides on manifesting, lowering anxiety, and finding a lasting love relationship, this would be a great oil to use in meditation or wear throughout the day. It has a calming effect on the nerves, and—being a rose plant—it is known to help you get into the vibration of romance.

LAVENDER: This is an oil that will amplify the third eye and crown chakras to help you connect to your guides. It has a calming effect that has been widely used to aid in going into a deep meditative state. It is also known to be helpful in attracting love.

ROSEMARY: This oil helps activate the upper chakras and give you energy to meditate. It's good to use if you're suffering from burnout or fatigue. It is a protecting oil that can help dispel negative energy and is known to help connect you to your soul and the spirit world. It is known as a teacher herb, which can help you keep a spiritual perspective.

SAGE: This plant is one known to help with purification and creating a sacred meditation space. It helps remove negative, heavy energy from your energy field and allow your mind to be clear. If your aim is to heal with your guides, this plant ally will be great to work with.

SANDALWOOD: This earthy oil has been used as far back as the ancient Egyptian time for connecting to the divine and deceased loved ones. It can help purify your energy field, increase your ability to focus in meditation, and help you create a strong sense recall that will help you drop into meditation quicker each time you sit to connect to your guides.

SPEARMINT: This oil targets the throat chakra, helping create clarity and openness to the spirit world in order to receive clear messages. It also can help you focus in meditation by helping you purify your energy. This is also a good oil to use if you feel yourself getting drowsy in meditation.

Herbs can be used to harmonize your energy, activate specific chakras, and connect to the spirit world. Some herbs may interact with prescription drugs, and you should consult a physician to see if it is safe for you to consume. Some herbs are not advised for pregnant or nursing women.

To Enhance the Third Eye

MUGWORT (*Artemisia vulgaris*): This herb is used by metaphysicians to enhance intuition and lucid dreaming. It is also linked to the divine feminine and can be used to connect to goddess energy, such as the Greek goddess Artemis after which it is named.

To Enhance the Connection to the Higher Self

ST. JOHN'S WORT (*Hypericum perforatum*): This herb has been used to enhance connection to the divine masculine and gods with a masculine energy. It helps bring strength and wards off depression and negativity. It is also used as a protective herb.

To Open Communication to Spirit

LICORICE (*Glycyrrhiza glabra*): This herb enhances your intention and can be used to open the throat chakra, which is how spirit guides communicate to you. If you are working on manifesting with your guides, this can help.

To Open the Crown Chakra

ROSE (*Rosoideae*): This love-enhancing herb can be used to connect to goddess energy and open you to the divine feminine. Its sweet essence enhances the function of the crown and heart chakras, opening you to self-love and the loving guidance of spirit helpers.

To Aid in Focus for Meditation

YERBA MATE (*Ilex paraguariensis*): This herb, known as the "drink of the gods," is linked to masculine deities and can provide you with the vitality to meditate and focus. It has been used to increase life-force energy since ancient times in South America.

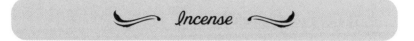

Burning incense is an ancient traditional meditation tool that can greatly enhance your ability to connect with your spirit guides. There are many incense options, and you can choose one intuitively or use one of the scents listed below that are known to aid in spiritual work.

ALOESWOOD: Also known as agarwood, this is one of the revered scents in Asian monasteries. It's associated with masculine energy as it invigorates you and clears your mind. It is known to help connect one to a state of transcendence and activate the third eye. It helps all of the upper chakras as well.

COPAL: This resin incense is great for clearing the vibration of your space throughout the day to keep you in an uplifted state. It hails from Central and South America and has been used in sacred spaces since ancient times to help connect to the Divine and manifest. You can also use it to clear your crystals.

FRANKINCENSE: There is hardly a more widely used incense for connecting to the Divine. This is both an ancient and modern incense known to help transcend the ego and put one in a relaxed yet concentrated state. It is also known to purify the space you want to meditate in.

JASMINE: This ancient Egyptian flower offers you an altered state of mind that melts sadness and can connect you to the unconditional love of angels and faeries. It is helpful for attracting love and luck. It is associated with the divine feminine energy as well.

ROSE: This incense invokes the divine feminine and can be used to connect to goddess energy for manifesting love and fertility. It is great for healing, feeling self-love, and opening to new growth and blessings.

SPIKENARD: This rare grounding incense is good for protecting your energy field from negativity. It can help you journey to the spirit realms and connect with your divine teachers. Set your intention as you light the incense to amplify its effects.

VANILLA: This is another incense known to activate the heart chakra and help one feel self-love to then attract more loving relationships. It can help if you struggle with sadness or codependency and want to focus more on your spiritual identity. It can amplify your intention to connect with spirit guides.

Just as the nose is a powerful way to trigger the mind to get into a meditative state, the ears can help us too. The vibration of sound has been used just as long as the power of scent to help as a tool for meditation and connection to the Divine. These instruments are less known in the West and can offer you assistance in working with your guides.

CHIME: A metal chime can be placed in your meditation space, and the high-pitch frequency of it can help both clear the space as well as help activate your crown chakra. Higher pitches resonate at the top of the head, and using a chime can help signal your brain to get into a meditative state each time.

DRUM: Used in shamanic traditions, drums can help create a trancelike state that allows the active mind to cease its circling so you can experience the divine states of consciousness. Beating a drum in a rhythmic manner can help you achieve deep meditation and connect to spirit guides.

GONG: Popular in Asia and growing in popularity in the West, the gong is a sacred tool that can help clear the energy field of negativity. It is to be played with reverence, not too loud and only from the edges. Gongs help soothe the nerves and restore the harmonic resonance of the body's energy field. It helps the subtle energy field by relieving psychic pressure caused by patterns of negative or fear-based thinking.

The gong is struck with a soft mallet in a rhythmic manner.

QUARTZ CRYSTAL BOWLS: Similar to the metal bowls, these crystal bowls are known to clear the energy for your meditation space. They come in different tones that target specific chakras and in different crystal variations, making their prices vary. They are great ways to restore your energy after periods of stress and can help you keep a daily meditation practice that is deep and transformational.

RATTLE: A rattle is another shamanic tool that disrupts the circling of the mind to help create a transcendent state. Use your intention to ask your spirit guides to connect to you and use the rattle to clear the space around you to prepare for meditation.

TIBETAN SINGING BOWL: This is a quick way to clear the energy in your meditation space before you begin to sit with your guides. If your space is used for multiple purposes, this would help clear the residual energy brought in by you and others so you can start with a neutral space. The bowl is struck with a wooden stick wrapped in soft suede to make a toning sound or a wooden stick is used to create a harmonic frequency by rubbing it smoothly along the edge.

Props

Being comfortable and having spinal alignment has been linked to deeper states of meditation by yogis for a very long time. These props can help you so that your energy can flow up the spine while you meditate and so you can relax without straining your muscles.

BENCH: For those with tight hamstrings, hips, or knees, a low meditation bench can help you keep your spine straight in meditation so that your lower back doesn't hurt. This provides support for the skeletal frame so you will stay in deep meditation and not fidget as much.

CUSHION: One of the most widely used tools for meditation is a simple firm cushion to sit on that elevates the hips. The feet remain on the floor as you sit in a cross-legged position. If you have flexibility, one way to sit is to turn the tops of the feet down and heels up so the heels rest at the perineum, knees rest on the floor, and you sit on the edge of the cushion.

EYE PILLOW: If you choose to meditate lying down, you may want an eye pillow, which helps block out sensory stimulation as well as bring energy to the third eye with a gentle pressure. This is commonly used in meditation portions of yoga classes. It can be made with beans and a sock as long as it isn't too heavy.

FOUNTAINS: The sound of moving water can help you stay relaxed for meditation, and moving water also helps clear the air by producing negative ions that help the nerves relax. Nature has prana that can help balance, clear, and charge your energy field.

SHAWL: Shawls made of organic fibers such as cotton, wool, or silk are often used to help hold a vibration that can build up over time. The feeling of being wrapped and cozy can help you relax as well.

Bibliography

Ananda Sangha Worldwide. "Paramahansa Yogananda and the Path of Kriya Yoga." 2015. https://www.paramhansayogananda.com/.

Ancient-Symbols. "Celtic Knots—History and Symbolism." Accessed April 22, 2022. https://www.ancient-symbols.com/celtic-knots.html.

———. "Triple Moon Symbol." Accessed April 22, 2022. https://www.ancient-symbols.com/symbols-directory/triple-moon.html.

BBC. "Spiritualism at a Glance." September 22, 2009. https://www.bbc.co.uk/religion/religions/spiritualism/ataglance/glance.shtml.

Bengal, Rebecca. "One Photographer's Exploration of the Paranormal." *New York Times*, October 31, 2019. https://www.nytimes.com/2019/10/31/t-magazine/seance-photos-shannon-taggart.html.

Cartwright, Mark. "Kali." *Ancient History Encyclopedia*, June 21, 2013. https://www.ancient.eu/Kali/.

Catholic Online. "St. Christopher." Accessed April 22, 2022. https://www.catholic.org/saints/saint.php?saint_id=36.

———. "St. Francis of Assisi." Accessed April 22, 2022. https://www.catholic.org/saints/saint.php?saint_id=50.

Chiorazzi, Anthony. "The Spirituality of Africa." *The Harvard Gazette*, October 6, 2015. https://news.harvard.edu/gazette/story/2015/10/the-spirituality-of-africa/.

Dhwty. "Eye of Horus: The True Meaning of an Ancient, Powerful Symbol." *Ancient Origins*, November 18, 2018. https://www.ancient-origins.net/artifacts-other-artifacts/eye-horus-0011014.

Editors of Encyclopaedia Britannica. "Dhyani-Buddha." Accessed April 22, 2022. https://www.britannica.com/topic/Dhyani-Buddha.

———. "Tara." Accessed April 22, 2022. https://www.britannica.com/topic/Tara-Buddhist-goddess.

Ferre, Lux. "Caduceus." *Occult World*, September 26, 2017. https://occult-world.com/caduceus/.

———. "Oshun." *Occult World*, November 13, 2017. https://occult-world.com/oshun/.

Gaelic Matters. "Celtic Knot Symbols." Accessed April 22, 2022. https://www.gaelicmatters.com/celtic-knot-symbols.html.

Gaia Staff. "Who Are the Pleiadians?" *Gaia*. December 2, 2020. https://www.gaia.com/article/who-are-the -pleiadians.

Heister, Kayce. "What Is a Mesa/Shamanic Altar?" *Modern Witch Doctor*, May 23, 2019. https://modernwitchdoctor.com/blog/f/growing-your -mesa?blogcategory=Spiritual+health.

Hodus, Lewis. "Buddhism and Buddhists in China." September 2003. http://www.authorama.com /buddhism-and-buddhists-in-china-4.html.

Hopler, Whitney. "Archangel Metatron's Cube in Sacred Geometry." *Learn Religions*, May 23, 2019. https://www.learnreligions.com/archangel-metatrons -cube-in-sacred-geometry-124293.

———. "Meet Archangel Chamuel, Angel of Peaceful Relationships." *Learn Religions*, February 20, 2019. https://www.learnreligions.com/meet-archangel -chamuel-124076.

Light Ascension. "Ascended Masters—Archangels and Cosmic Beings." Accessed April 22, 2022. https://www .lightascension.com/arts/Ascended%20Master.htm.

Magner, Erin. "This Is What The OM Symbol Means, In Case You Were Wondering." *Well and Good*, January 16, 2019. https://www.wellandgood.com/om-symbol -meaning/.

Mark, Joshua J. "The Ankh." *Ancient History Encyclopedia*, September 19, 2016. https://www.ancient.eu/Ankh/.

———. "The Life of Hercules in Myth and Legend." *Ancient History Encyclopedia*, July 23, 2014. https://www.ancient.eu/article/733/the-life-of -hercules-in-myth--legend/.

O'Brien, Barbara. "The Wheel of Life." *Learn Religions*, December 21, 2018. https://www.learnreligions.com /the-wheel-of-life-4123213.

Original Botanica. "The Magic of the Seven African Powers." September 7, 2021. https://www.original botanica.com/blog/seven-african-powers-orishas -rituals-spells/.

Religion Facts. "Buddhas." January 10, 2017. http://www.religionfacts.com/buddha.

Sacred Fire. "Celtic Shamanism." 21 January 2000. https://www.sacredfire.net/shaman.html.

Self-Realization Fellowship. "Mahavatar Babaji." Accessed April 22, 2022. https://yogananda.org/mahavatar -babaji.

TOI Astrology. "Know the 8 Benefits You Can Gain by Worshiping Lord Ganesha." *Times of India*, July 24, 2019. https://timesofindia.indiatimes.com/astrology /hindu-mythology/know-the-8-benefits-you-can-gain-by -worshiping-lord-ganesha/articleshow/70356746.cms.

Token Rock. "Flower of Life." Accessed April 22, 2022. https://www.tokenrock.com/explain-flower-of-life-46 .html.

Top China Travel. "Chinese Dragon Worship." Accessed April 22, 2022. https://www.topchinatravel.com/china -guide/chinese-dragon-worship.htm.

Virtue, Doreen. "8 Signs from Archangel Raphael." Belief Net. Accessed April 22, 2022. https://www.beliefnet .com/inspiration/angels/2010/06/healing-miracles-of -archangel-raphael.aspx.

Wigington, Patti. "Deities of Ancient Egypt." *Learn Religions*, June 10, 2018. https://www.learnreligions .com/deities-of-ancient-egypt-2561794.

———. "Gods of the Celts." *Learn Religions*. December 24, 2018. https://www.learnreligions.com/gods -of-the-celts-2561711.

To Write to the Author

If you wish to contact the author or would like more information about this book, please write to the author in care of Llewellyn Worldwide and we will forward your request. Both the author and the publisher appreciate hearing from you and learning of your enjoyment of this book and how it has helped you. Llewellyn Worldwide cannot guarantee that every letter written to the author can be answered, but all will be forwarded. Please write to:

Shannon Yrizarry
℅ Llewellyn Worldwide
2143 Wooddale Drive
Woodbury, MN 55125-2989

Please enclose a self-addressed stamped envelope for reply or $1.00 to cover costs. If outside the USA, enclose an international postal reply coupon.

Many of Llewellyn's authors have websites with additional information and resources. For more information, please visit our website:

WWW.LLEWELLYN.COM